» Homeworkers in
Global Perspective «

» Homeworkers in Global Perspective «

Invisible No More

edited by

Eileen Boris

and

Elisabeth Prügl

Routledge   New York & London

Published in 1996 by

Routledge
29 West 35th Street
New York, NY 10001

Published in Great Britain by

Routledge
11 New Fetter Lane
London EC4P 4EE

Library of Congress Cataloging-in-Publication Data available from the
Library of Congress

To Rhonda Boris, in sisterhood

—E. B.

To my parents, Hans and Loni Prügl

—E. P.

Contents »

List of Illustrations »

Acknowledgments »

First, we would like to thank each other and our authors for making this volume possible. We have each benefited from the other's enthusiasm when our own has sagged under the weight of other commitments. We would like to thank Cecelia Cancellaro and the staff at Routledge for their work on this volume. The Renvall Institute for Historical Studies, University of Helsinki, the Department of History at Howard University, the School of International Service at The American University, and the Department of International Relations at Florida International University aided our efforts through fax machines and other support services. José Alonso, Jane Tate, Minna Salmi, Lucita Lazo, and the ILO office in Washington helped us find photographs. Faranak Miraftab, Anita Weiss, Jaime Silva/Ênfase and Lisa Sakulensky permitted us to reprint their photographs. Weiguo Yin compiled the bibliography and hunted down missing information without fail.

We have both gained support from funding agencies. Eileen would like to thank the Ford Foundation for sending her to India in 1989. There she met Renana Jhabvala and Ela Bhatt of SEWA, who remain inspirations for us all. She also acknowledges grants from the Woodrow Wilson International Center for Scholars and the Museum of American History, Smithsonian Institution, that allowed her to research home-based work in the United States and explore the international context along the way. She also thanks the J. William Fulbright Commission for sending her to Finland as coholder of the Bicentennial Chair in American Studies at the University of Helsinki for 1993–1994. In Finland she met Minna Salmi and had the opportunity to lecture about home-based work outside the United States. She appreciated the effort of Jane Tate to arrange her meeting with other homeworker organizers and homeworkers in Leeds in March 1994, a meeting that became part of a lecture tour that included discussions with Sheila Allen, Carol Wolkowitz, and other researchers in Great Britain. She also thanks Sheila Rowbotham and Swasti Mitter for their work on homeworker organizing; she appreciates their support over the years. Finally, Eileen acknowledges her debt to Nelson Lichtenstein, whose work continues to provide a model of engaged scholarship. Dan Lichtenstein-Boris absented himself at summer camp during a crucial period of manuscript preparation.

Lisa would like to thank the School of International Service at The American University for doctoral fellowships that made possible her research on the global politics of home-based work. She is also grateful to the American Association of University Women for supporting her with an American Fellowship while she was writing her dissertation. A postdoctoral fellowship from the School of International Service at The American University enabled her to carry out editorial work for this book, prepare one of her own chapters, and organize round tables of homeworker advocates for the 1991 AWID Forum. She would like to thank Nicholas Onuf, Renée Marlin-Bennett, and Robert Gregg for their encouragement and constructive feedback on various drafts of her dissertation. She is grateful to Gisela Schneider de Villegas, who provided her with access to ILO files on home-based work and helped arrange her stay at the ILO in Geneva. Many thanks also to Jane Tate, who never tired of sharing her meticulous reports on the homeworkers she visited and on meetings she attended around the world. Lisa is also indebted to Irene Tinker for her unfailing support and friendship and for sparking her interest in home-based work. Peter Cattan gave helpful feedback on a variety of issues, assisted with translations from Spanish and Portuguese, and provided love and support throughout this endeavor

Part One »

« **Overview**

1 »

Introduction

« *Elisabeth Prügl and Eileen Boris*

"THOSE WHO HAVE BEEN MARGINALIZED ARE NOW ENTERING THE MAINSTREAM," Ela Bhatt announced at the 1991 Meeting of Experts on the Social Protection of Homeworkers in Geneva organized by the International Labour Organisation (ILO). General secretary of the Self Employed Women's Association (SEWA) of India and a leader in the international struggle to gain recognition, better wages, and social security for homeworkers, Bhatt was reading the signs of the time. Wage earning at home has entered the arena of international politics. The subject has occupied the Council of Europe, which issued a report titled "The Protection of Persons Working at Home" in 1989, and the European Union (EU), which published a task force report called "Homeworking in the EC" in 1994. The issue has also become part of the ILO agenda, and the ILO has led the international discussion on home-based work. It has organized regional conferences in Asia and Latin America, debated the topic at the Meeting of Experts in Geneva, and at its 1995 annual meeting of member states considered establishing an international labor standard on home-based work.[1]

Home-based work has appeared on the international agenda before. What distinguishes the current debate from that in the first half of this century is the voices and participation of homeworkers themselves. In March 1994, representatives of homeworker advocacy groups from countries around the world met in Brussels and established an umbrella organization called Homenet International. One of the organization's objectives is "to coordinate an international campaign for the improvement of home-based workers' conditions of work at national, regional and international levels,"[2] and its establishment crowned several years of networking; international meetings in Europe, Asia, and the United States; and get-togethers at ILO conferences.

We were privileged to witness and participate in the formation of this international homeworker movement; this collection is one outcome of our involvement. In April 1989, Eileen Boris attended an international conference sponsored by the Ford Foundation and the ILO in Ahmedabad, India. The meeting sought to assess current knowledge about homeworking and to encourage further research as a necessary step toward the development of an international convention. Eileen provided information on home-based work and labor laws in the United States that grew out of her historical studies but incorporated recent trends. At this event, she met a number of activists working with homeworkers as well as researchers from Asia, Latin America, the Middle East, and Africa. At that time Elisabeth (Lisa) Prügl, who was beginning work on a dissertation exploring the international politics of home-based work, approached Eileen, who was able to provide her with the names of people she had met in Ahmedabad.

Lisa attended the first international meeting organized by nongovernmental organizations (NGOs) which brought homeworker advocates to the Netherlands in May 1990. As part of her efforts to collect data from the ILO, she also participated in the 1991 Meeting of Experts on the Social Protection of Homeworkers in Geneva. For the 1991 Forum of the Association of Women in Development (AWID), Lisa organized two roundtables that brought together researchers, homeworker advocates, and union representatives. Roundtable participants discussed the possibility of formalizing an international network; the idea of this book was born at that forum. The book is a contribution to action research: a sharing of knowledge with the goal of aiding homeworkers in the international struggle for recognition and empowerment.

As the international discussion of home-based work brings together the experiences of women both in the capitalist center and in the periphery, one of the most intractable problems it encounters is that of definition. In their definition of home-based work, Western authors include primarily industrial and various forms of clerical homework. However, grassroots organizers in India maintain that such workers are only one subcategory of the larger group of the "self-employed" in the informal sector who all share similar problems. These differences express themselves in this collection in the terminologies writers tend to adopt. Scholars focusing on highly industrialized areas (Europe, North America, large cities in the South such as Rio) prefer the term *homework*, but those who study rural economies tend to use the term *home-based work*[3] because their conceptual frame of reference is the informal sector in its diverse forms, not necessarily work relations under industrial capitalism. Yet the distinction between home-based wage earners and the self-employed is getting less pronounced in "postindustrial" economies, as the case of Finland shows.

The ILO has proposed to define homework as "the production of goods or the provision of services for an employer or contractor under an arrangement whereby the work is carried out at the place of the worker's own choosing, often the worker's own home. It is normally carried out without direct supervision by the employer or contractor."[4] Here the emphasis is not so much on the home as workplace as on the fact that the work is carried out on behalf of someone else, albeit not under the direct supervision of the work giver. The ILO definition excludes self-employed workers who do not depend on someone else to give them a job. But, as Prügl points out in Chapter 11, "Biases in Labor Law," dependence is often a matter of degree, and home-based workers come in a variety of forms. For instance, they may provide their own tools and some raw materials but depend on a trader for other inputs and a market outlet. In India, employers in the *bidi* industry have resorted to a "sale-purchase system" in order to uphold the fiction that home-based workers are self-employed. They sell tobacco and leaves to bidi rollers and buy back the cigarettes once they are finished. This practice resembles the classification of home typists as independent contractors by insurance companies in the United States.[5] In all such systems, women are more likely to be dependent because of gender ideologies and divisions of labor that prevent them from becoming truly independent entrepreneurs. This collection focuses on the types of home-based workers who are involved in subcontracting arrangements or who are dependent on traders to some extent. But, as some chapters in Part III show, opening avenues toward entrepreneurship can be an important strategy in empowering homeworkers.

The surge of interest in home-based work since the beginning of the 1990s has not happened in a vacuum. Structural changes in the organization of international capitalism are detrimentally affecting women's economic position. Characteristic of these changes is a progressive decentralization of production processes, including their geographic dispersal around the world, a pattern that has been described as the "global assembly line." Companies roam the globe in search of the most profitable production arrangements, but they centralize control of such processes in what Saskia Sassen calls "global cities" such as New

York, London, or Tokyo. This international restructuring leads to changes in class because, by resorting to "flexible" subcontracting arrangements, companies are gradually eliminating a middle class of (largely male) production workers in center economies who in the post–World War II era had achieved wages that supported a family, job guarantees, and benefits ensuring their social security. In place of this middle class, a disproportionately female work force is taking over jobs in export-processing plants in newly industrializing countries (NICs). In addition, subcontracting chains are drawing homeworkers and other workers in the informal sector into international production in rich as well as poor nations. These workers are mostly women and immigrants. They form one extreme in the sharpening polarization of the labor force into those who benefit from the ongoing restructuring and "global control capability" and those who are left with so-called flexible work arrangements; who are paid low wages; who receive no benefits; and who find themselves cut out of social security, labor standards, and other state guarantees.[6] In Latin America and Asia, some governments have adopted policies that accelerate these processes. In response to structural adjustment programs, economic crises, and pressure to repay large foreign debts, they deregulate labor markets and open up their economies. In order to compete in the international markets, national companies resort increasingly to subcontracting, drawing in cheap female labor and putting out work to the home based.[7]

Homeworker organizing against such forces would not have occured without the new international women's movement, which is raising awareness that women's work has the same value as men's, even when it is carried out at home. Feminists are leading efforts to organize homeworkers in India, England, and Canada. Feminists in unions have insisted that homeworkers have a place equal to traditional union members. Feminists in the ILO have proposed projects to support homeworker organizing and have lobbied to place home-based work on the agenda of the international labor conference. Finally, feminists have studied and publicized the experiences of homeworkers.[8]

Three bodies of thought are especially pertinent to locating homeworkers in academic discourse: those regarding women and work, women in development (WID), and gender and social policy. Feminist scholarship has transformed the ways that we think about work, (re)charting geographies of labor and in the process (re)portraying who is a worker. The wage no longer divides worker from nonworker. Feminist scholars now view as work activities once classified by Marxists as reproduction, as opposed to the production that extracts surplus labor from the waged worker. Work includes family and community labor devalued under capitalist industrialization: housework, child care and dependent care, sex/affective production, voluntary activities—what socialist feminists labeled social reproduction, those services that maintain people daily and intergenerationally. In tandem with anti-imperialist, anticolonial, and subaltern studies, feminist scholars have shifted the focus from the Western capitalist center to other organizations of labor dismissed by the center as primitive forms associated with the household—itself devalued as the arena of unpaid labor performed by women and connected to the realm of necessity. In the crevices of the everyday, we have found work that is just as significant to social life as any other form of labor. In doing so, we have stretched the spaces of labor from the factory or shop floor to include the home, family, and neighborhood. The worker no longer appears as the blue-collar male proletarian, or even the white-collar female typist, prototypical gendered occupations associated with the capitalist core. By naming home-based activities *work*, we expose the gendered and regional nature of the categories through which scholarship reconstructs the world.[9]

The topic of home-based work particularly illuminates the permeable quality of such conceptual boundaries. Located in the space of the family, in the dwelling, such work brings the wage into the place where "love," "duty," and "need"—themselves problematic terms—compel labor. Like work outside the household, home-based work depends on sexual divisions of labor and gender constructions, as Boris argues in Chapter 2. Waged labor at home has shared the invisibility of housework: Both have belonged to a larger gendered structuring of employment in which occupations, as well as the processes and places of labor, become designated either male or female. Employers have structured work to take advantage of sexual divisions and gender ideology. They pay women less because women belong in the home, and this self-perpetuating prophecy intensifies the structural barriers that women often face in seeking waged labor. With family and domestic labor largely or solely theirs to perform, mothers around the world find it difficult to earn wages according to scripts written with the unencumbered man in mind as the ideal worker. Those who find themselves tied to the household seek remuneration there, in "women's place."[10]

Scholarship on WID composes one strand of the vast literature on women and work. Countering years of neglect by international development agencies, this research documents the extent of "Third World" women's work, much of it home based and including unpaid activities such as food processing, fetching firewood and water, caring for children, and community work as well as income-earning activities such as crafts production, street vending, and industrial homework. The biases of development planners and labor statisticians have kept this kind of work from public discussion. WID literature reveals the double edge of women's home-based income earning: on the one hand, women stretch their working day to combine paid work and household tasks, often suffering from exploitation by employers, family, and themselves; on the other hand, they earn much-needed income, gain self-confidence, and sometimes improve their social status.[11]

In the context of industrial restructuring and the economic crises of the 1980s, WID researchers have begun to relate women's economic position to the structure of unequal labor markets. They have adduced models of a new international division of labor and a reorganization of production that increasingly incorporates subcontracting in order to save costs and raise profits. They have located the role of women at the intersection of the new international division of labor and a gendered division of labor as, in an effort to save costs and increase profits, international capitalists have drawn on the cheap labor of "Third World" women—ideologically constructed as nimble-fingered and docile. A wide range of studies have connected subcontracting chains, homeworkers, and export increases.[12]

Exploring the effects of the economic crisis since the 1980s and of structural adjustment policies on the well-being of women and their families, many researchers around the globe have described the strategies households employ to make up for lost earnings, welfare benefits, and deteriorating buying power. Their location in the capitalist periphery, gender divisions of labor, and gender ideologies mold women's and men's options. For women, restructuring and economic reform often mean more unpaid work as they stretch household resources and compensate for care previously provided by the state. In addition, they participate more actively in the labor force, frequently in the informal sector, because their options in the formal sector are limited. Home-based work is a significant strategy for many as they seek to combine their increased domestic responsibilities with a dire need to earn income. Household strategies reproduce gender inequality; however, households are also fields of contestation in which relationships are being negotiated, and the current economic restructuring entails a renegotiating (though not necessarily a reversal) of power relationships as reflected in patterns of income allocation, the distribution of unpaid household labor, and differences in bargaining power.[13]

State policies are crucial in determining the contours of the homework system. Over the past fifteen years, social scientists have striven to bring the state back into our analysis of work and family life, and home-based work belongs to the larger study of social and economic policy. As it breaks down the dichotomy between work and family, it also reveals the connections among labor policy, family policy, and a host of other macro- and microeconomic decisions. Definitions of *worker* for the purposes of labor standards, social insurance, and social security policies determine conditions of homeworking. Rules governing taxation, housing, export, foreign investment, labor relations, and immigration, among other things, shape the environment under which home-based work develops. Hidden in the home, homeworkers have remained outside social policy as workers, but as mothers and community members they have sometimes become the target of social programs, as case studies in Part III of this book reveal. Gender analysis has transformed our study of the state so that social and economic policy have become an arena in which conceptions of womanhood and manhood, as well as the power of men over women and of more-privileged women over less-privileged ones, are constructed and reconstructed. But women have become actors in this new scholarship—a transformation in discourse that reflects shifts in international politics exemplified by the interventions of homeworkers in the debate over the conditions of their labor. As Sheila Rowbotham and Swasti Mitter have documented, homeworker organizing belongs to a worldwide effort by poor women to improve their lives.[14]

Overview of the Chapters

The genesis of this collection explains its contents. In trying to assemble illustrative case studies, we drew upon the developing international network of homework advocates and researchers. We sought to represent the major regions of the world where homeworking and homeworker organization are taking place. We were not always successful; we would have liked to include an essay from the Netherlands and one on immigrant communities in the United States. But we sought to move away from the well-explored cases, such as that of SEWA, to focus on less-known but equally compelling examples. Our one essay on the United States situates itself within the framework of rural development studies, a necessary corrective to the usual consideration of the U.S. as a core capitalist economy. Most of our authors come from the areas they write on; many are not native speakers of English. When necessary, we have reworked prose while retaining individual authorial voices; similarly, we have tried to maintain the kinds of markings that a predominantly U.S. audience expects from such essays without sacrificing the different scholarly traditions in which our authors write. Some homeworker activists were unable to meet our deadlines, but we have assembled a representative sample of cases to contribute to the international dialogue on home-based work.

We have divided this collection into three parts. Part I consists of this introduction and two overview essays. Chapter 2, Boris's historical synthesis, suggests how home-based work developed as part of the Western industrialization process, different from cottage industry but connected to the domestic economy. She argues that sexual divisions of labor and gendered conventions were crucial both to the contours of the homework system and to attempts to regulate it in the United States, Great Britain, Germany, and France. In this chapter we see the historical roots of dichotomies—mother and worker, home and work—that persist in the current debate. In Chapter 3, Prügl discusses home-based work in terms of the evolving literature on women, work, and development. She describes the WID literature, resultant programs, and critiques that recognize how the global capitalist economy influences the shape of women's work, especially in the "Third World." Critiques of neoliberalism and of the categories through which development is constructed lead to a gendered analysis in which power relationships—between core and periphery, men and women, employers and workers—demand consideration. Rather than empowering women, development relies on "the oppressor's language," creating the idea of a homogeneous "Third World woman" that denies the multiplicity of experiences constituting homeworker lives.

The case studies in Part II explore the diverse experiences of housewives, mothers, and workers who earn wages at home. These chapters derive from fieldwork, interviews, survey data, and economic and social analysis. All situate homeworking both in gender relations and in the larger political economy of an industry, locality, or nation-state. Just as the garment industry lends itself to home-based work throughout the world, so it dominates these examples, whether in the Americas or in Asia. A range of skill runs through such home-based work, from the high-fashion sewing of Rio de Janeiro to the cheap clothes of Zapotlanejo. The crafts skill of the Iranian carpetmaker, the "crude" or "refined" sewing skills of Javanese village women, and the expertise of Brazilian seamstresses challenge conventional understandings of skill that devalue what those women learned in the process of becoming women. In Finland, which has an advanced capitalist economic base, home-based work exists in 290 census categories. Child minding as a municipal employee is a major form of home-based work for women, in sharp contrast to the work of more typical garment laborers in other areas of the world.

The voices of homeworkers come alive in these studies. We see homeworkers in their multiple identities and watch how this predominately female labor force finds survival and flexibility, fulfillment and exploitation in home-based work. As Alice Rangel de Paiva Abreu and Bila Sorj argue in Chapter 6, homeworkers are active agents in the construction of their lives, not the victims of larger economic or social forces. Nonetheless, gender ideologies, at times connected to religious worldviews such as Brazilian Evangelicalism and Iranian Islam, restrict their lives, and homeworkers negotiate their diverse responsibilities within the boundaries of the domestic and family realm.

These studies are about women, but they are also about gender as a construct and as a material force. Chapter 4, by Faranak Miraftab, and Chapter 9, by Minna Salmi, compare the experiences of men and women to provide fresh insights into the gendered meaning of home-based labor. Miraftab also advances our understanding of the spatial dimension of home-based work. In her analysis of the spatial juxtaposition of productive and reproductive labor, we witness how men and women arrange their work spaces to reflect the self-perceptions of male producers and breadwinners and female housewives and helpmates. Though culture, economics, and geography separate Finland from Mexico, Salmi finds that men do not alter their patterns of work even when they are in the home, a conclusion confirmed in Chapter 10, Gringeri's study of homeworkers in the midwestern United States. These studies reveal that male homeworkers and nonhomeworking men treat time, space, and earnings similarly, whereas women homeworkers arrange their space as well as their time for greater flexibility to meet their dual role. In Mexico, the spatial merging of family and wage earning enables women to fulfill reproductive as well as productive labor but at the cost of making their contribution to the family economy invisible.

In Chapter 5, Anita M. Weiss finds a similar outcome in the Pakistani Walled City of Lahore, where women's confinement not only hides their labor but limits their employment options. Her spatial analysis extends from the household to the neighborhood and beyond. Here religion and respectability set boundaries for gender- and class-derived survival strategies. Home-based work might empower its practitioners if women controlled the materials and marketing instead of falling under the power of male employers and family intermediaries.

The Brazilian women studied in Chapter 6 could also maintain their respectability by staying at home while sewing for income. Few had separate spaces for their home-based work. As in Mexico, where the culture of *machismo* persists, men failed to help with manual family labor, although some of the Brazilian women hired maids for child care and household maintenance. Though they possess a talent, these women think of their work in terms of income gained rather than career advanced because they regard their work in terms of the family rather than as an independent aspect of their individuality. Because of its low position in the hierarchy of work, home-based work fails to provide greater power within the family. With this study, Rangel de Paiva Abreu and Sorj significantly advance our understanding of the subjective experience of homeworking in relation to its structural context.

In Chapter 7, so does Zohreh Ghavamshahidi, whose fieldwork in two Iranian villages confirms that Iranian gender ideology led to the feminization of home-based work. Here too girls learned their skill as part of their socialization, in the process of becoming women. Dependent on contractors, weavers lacked control over the labor process; even independent weavers, who had greater autonomy, funneled their earnings into the family. Capitalist development joins a reconstituted Iranian patriarchy to obscure the productive labor of these housewives and mothers because it occurs in the home.

Women in rural Java have internalized gender ideologies to such an extent that they pretend their husbands are the "main workers," as Dewi Haryani Susilastuti illustrates in Chapter 8. Although they do most of the home-based work, women are considered mere "helpers," together with other family members. As in other cases, home-based work in this rural setting is one survival strategy among many. But, in contrast to most urban cases, it usually involves several household members, and households derive the bulk of their income from garment assembly. Susilastuti's case study provides a vivid document of informalization, of entrepreneurs struggling in a volatile market, laying off their inworkers, i.e. workers they employ in workshops or factories, in order to save costs and failing to raise piece rates over the course of a ten year period, with all the hardship this entails for workers.

In Chapter 9, Salmi debunks the "myths of homeworking," showing that not all homeworkers in Finland are mothers of small children forced by a lack of choice into such labor. Her chapter suggests the possibilities of homeworking under advanced capitalism, and it simultaneously exposes the informalization at the center of "postindustrial" restructuring. Yet even in Finland, where the welfare state provides services for women and women have perhaps the highest full-time labor force participation in the world, homeworkers earn less than their counterparts who labor in other locations.

In institutionalizing routines and in providing a forum for engagement and conflict, the state (re)creates the homeworking system with its ideological constructs of gender. Part III of this book addresses the practices of governments at international, national, and local levels in (re)creating home-based work as a marginal, supplemental, low-paid activity and the emerging efforts of homeworker organizations to counter such practices. In Chapters 11 and 12, Elisabeth Prügl and Jeanne Hahn illustrate the importance of the internationalized state in this process of governmental reinforcement of gender constructs. They show how homeworkers remain outside labor law on a global level and how World Bank and International Monetary Fund (IMF) policies of economic liberalization turn Indian women into cheap, informal sector workers. In Chapter 10, Christina Gringeri describes the workings of the state at the local level, where "private development corporations" made up of businessmen, bankers, and other leading male community members—with financial support from state governments—have designed low-paid auto assembly work specifically for farmers' wives while creating stable factory jobs for men. Gringeri explores home-based work as a development strategy in declining farming communities. She illustrates how the ideological assumptions of company officials, local leaders, and the local population interact to construct home-based work as an ideal supplementary income opportunity for farm women. In addition to the ideological construction of homeworkers as nonworkers documented in Part II, the practices of the state in the rural midwestern United States cement an understanding of home-based work as marginal employment. In contrast, the Finnish state has given home-based work more central status by creating a home-based occupation, municipal child minding.

Central to constructions of homeworkers as marginal is the practice of treating them as self-employed. According to Prügl, ambiguities in labor laws—erected on the model of the factory and office worker—make this miscategorization possible. Legal tests of "employee" status assume that workers are in an employer-owned space where an employer always can supervise them. This definition excludes homeworkers. Furthermore, such tests assume a specific form of dichotomy between employer and employee and therefore obscure the multiple degrees of dependency characteristic of the "atypical" forms of work women engage in.

States also affect homeworkers through economic policies. Jeanne Hahn explores this impact in the Indian state, documenting the symbiotic and changing relationship between the informal and the formal sectors. Women lost ground in home-based crafts production and their rates of labor force participation dropped as a result of British colonial policies and the push toward large-scale industrialization in the post-Independence period. They have since gained ground in the export-oriented garment industry, and industrial homework has proliferated. Women now make up the bulk of workers in the informal sector, but government statistics obscure women's crucial contribution because they severely undercount women's work.

The Indian context has helped spawn some of the best-known examples of homeworker organizing. SEWA in Ahmedabad and the Working Women's Forum in Madras have provided an example and inspiration to homeworker organizations around the world. Both of these organizations emerged from a concern with workers in the informal sector. They provide a range of services using a variety of strategies, ranging from credit, training, cooperatives, and social insurance programs to public protest, bargaining with employers, and intermediation with labor inspectors.[15]

For both Alex Dagg (Chapter 13) and Lucita Lazo (Chapter 14), leaders in efforts to organize homeworkers in Canada and the Philippines, respectively, SEWA served as an example. Canadian union organizing of homeworkers has responded to the effects of industrial restructuring, accelerated by the Canada-

U.S. free trade accord. Dagg argues for a new type of unionism that draws on the experiences of grassroots organizations like SEWA. This "community unionism" seeks cooperation between unions and community groups, draws on ethnic networks—word of mouth and the media—and offers the union office as a quasi community center where workers can find social contact, English language classes, and neighborhood chats as well as legal advice, benefit plans, and informational seminars.

This rapprochement between grassroots organizing and unionism also lies at the center of Lazo's description of homeworker organizing in the Philippines and Jane Tate's portrait of the West Yorkshire Homeworking Unit (Chapter 15). Lazo coordinates an ILO project that supports the organizing effort in the Philippines. Because the ILO is an international organization, its approach is top-down by definition. But Lazo demonstrates the importance of involving a committed nongovernmental organization in such projects. With its proven strategies of community organizing, KaBaPa was perfectly suited to creating the core of a national homeworker association. Because of the ILO's role in the project, it was undoubtedly easier to win sections of the government as an ally than it was in Canada, where even a sympathetic government needed considerable pressure.

Tracing the multiple links between homeworker organizations, Tate reminds us of the value of an international outlook in a context where economies are becoming increasingly global and states orient their policies to global requirements. International contacts have fostered a diffusion of ideas and approaches and now support lobbying for international action on behalf of homeworkers. Tate insists that such contacts have to involve homeworkers themselves. Homeworkers in West Yorkshire have increased their self-confidence, created their own organization, and are planning to establish a business trading the goods of homeworkers from around the world.

Although academic analysis—of the policies of the local state in the U.S. or of international labor legislation and economic policies—casts the state as the problem, activists for homeworkers look to the state for solutions. They lobby for changes in labor laws, for an international labor standard, and for resources to support their organizing efforts. Academic analysis is combining with grassroots organizing in the political struggle of homeworkers to affirm their basic value and dignity and to achieve their rights as workers. In this process, women are re-creating themselves as powerful agents in control of their own fate.

Notes

1   "The Protection of Persons Working at Home" (Strasbourg: Council of Europe,

1989); Jane Tate, "Homeworking in the EC," report of the ad hoc Working Group on Homeworking (Brussels: European Commission, 1993); ILO, "Social Protection of Homeworkers: Documents of the Meeting of Experts on the Social Protection of Homeworkers" (Geneva: International Labor Office, 1990).

2   Homenet International, "Circular on International Network for Home-based Workers," mimeo, c. 1994.

3   In this introduction we use both *homeworkers* and *home-based work* in order to reflect this diversity. Authors of various chapters use the terms they find most appropriate.

4   International Labour Conference, *Home Work*, Report V (1), 82nd Session, 1995 (Geneva: International Labour Office, 1994), p. 5.

5   Renana Jhabvala and Reva Dhawan, "Bidi Homeworkers in Gujarat," in Renana Jhabvala, Reva Dhawan, and Krishan Mahajan, *Women Who Roll Bidis: Two Studies of Gujarat* (Ahmedabad: Self Employed Women's Association, 1985). Bidis are a type of cigarette. For a summary of white-collar, home-based labor and problems of definition, see Eileen Boris, *Home to Work: Motherhood and the Politics of Industrial Homework in the United States* (New York: Cambridge University Press, 1994), pp. 324–336.

6   Saskia Sassen, *The Global City: New York, London, Tokyo* (Princeton: Princeton University Press, 1991); see also Swasti Mitter, *Common Fate, Common Bond: Women in the Global Economy* (London: Pluto Press, 1986).

7   Guy Standing, "Global Feminization Through Flexible Labor," *World Development* 17 (July 1989): 1077–1095; Lourdes Benería and Shelley Feldman, *Unequal Burden: Economic Crises, Persistent Poverty, and Women's Work* (Boulder, Colo.: Westview Press, 1992).

8   Sheila Rowbotham and Swasti Mitter, eds., *Dignity and Daily Bread: New Forms of Economic Organising Among Poor Women in the Third World and the First* (London: Routledge, 1994); Sheila Rowbotham, *Homeworkers Worldwide* (London: Merlin Press, 1993).

9   The literature on women and work is vast. For some examples of these trends, see Heidi Hartmann, "The Unhappy Marriage of Marxism and Feminism: Towards a More Progressive Union," in *Women and Revolution: A Discussion of the Unhappy Marriage of Marxism and Feminism*, ed. Lydia Sargent (Boston: South End Press, 1981), pp. 1–41; Marilyn Waring, *If Women Counted: A New Feminist Economics* (New York: HarperCollins, 1988); Lourdes Benería, "Production, Reproduction, and the Sexual Division of Labor," *Cambridge Journal of Economics* 3 (September 1979): 203–225; Lisa Leghorn and Katherine Parker, *Women's Worth: Sexual Economics and the World of Women* (Boston: Routledge & Kegan Paul, 1981); Lourdes Benería and Catharine R. Stimpson, eds., *Women, Households, and the Economy* (New Brunswick, N.J.: Rutgers University Press, 1987); Jane L. Collins and Martha Gimenez, eds., *Work Without Wages: Domestic Labor and Self-Employment Within Capitalism* (Albany: State University of New York Press, 1990); and Kate Young, Carol Wolkowitz, and Roslyn McCullagh, *Of Marriage and the Market:*

Women's Subordination in International Perspective (London: CSE Books, 1981).

10 For previous studies of homework and women's casualized labor, see Eileen Boris and Cynthia R. Daniels, eds., *Homework: Historical and Contemporary Perspectives on Paid Labor at Home* (Urbana: University of Illinois Press, 1989); Boris, *Home to Work*; Sheila Allen and Carol Wolkowitz, *Homeworking: Myths and Realities* (London: Macmillan, 1987); Kathleen Christensen, *Women and Home-Based Work: The Unspoken Contract* (New York: Henry Holt and Company, 1988); Annie Phizacklea, *Unpacking the Fashion Industry: Gender, Racism, and Class in Production* (London: Routledge, 1990); Rowbotham and Mitter, *Dignity and Daily Bread*; and Rowbotham, *Homeworkers Worldwide*.

11 For examples of this literature, see Irene Tinker and Michelle Bo Bramsen, eds., *Women and World Development* (New York: Praeger, 1976); Barbara Rogers, *The Domestication of Women: Discrimination in Developing Societies* (London: Tavistock Publications, 1980); Sue Ellen M. Charlton, *Women in Third World Development* (Boulder, Colo.: Westview Press, 1984); Irene Tinker, ed., *Persistent Inequalities: Women and World Development* (New York: Oxford University Press, 1990); and Caroline O. N. Moser, *Gender Planning and Development: Theory, Practice and Training* (London: Routledge, 1993). For studies on home-based work, see Günseli Berik, *Women Carpet Weavers in Rural Turkey: Patterns of Employment, Earnings and Status* (Geneva: International Labour Office, 1987); Zarina Bhatty, *The Economic Role and Status of Women in the Beedi Industry in Allahabad, India* (Saarbrücken and Fort Lauderdale: Verlag Breitenbach Publishers, 1981); Maria Mies, *The Lace Makers of Narsapur: Indian Housewives Produce for the World Market* (London: Zed Press, 1982); and Andrea Menefee Singh and Anita Kelles-Viitanen, eds., *Invisible Hands: Women in Home-Based Production* (New Delhi: Sage Publications, 1987).

12 See June Nash and María Patricia Fernández-Kelly, eds., *Women, Men, and the International Division of Labor* (Albany: State University of New York Press, 1983); and Kathryn Ward, ed., *Women Workers and Global Restructuring* (Ithaca, N.Y.: ILR Press, 1990). For evidence on international subcontracting chains, including homeworkers, see Rukmini Rao and Sahba Husain, "Invisible Hands: Women in Home-Based Production in the Garment Export Industry in Delhi," in *Invisible Hands*, p. 51; Rosalinda Pineda-Ofreneo, "Philippine Domestic Outwork: Subcontracting for Export-Oriented Industries," *Journal of Contemporary Asia* 12, 3 (1982): 281–293; Swarna Jayaweera and Malsiri Dias, "Subcontracting in Industry: Impact on Women" (Colombo, Sri Lanka: Center for Women's Research, 1989); Lourdes Benería and Martha Roldán, *The Crossroads of Class and Gender: Industrial Homework, Subcontracting, and Household Dynamics in Mexico City* (Chicago: The University of Chicago Press, 1987); Rita Gallin, "Women and the Export Industry in Taiwan: The Muting of Class Consciousness," in *Women Workers and Global Restructuring*, pp. 179–192; and Maria de los Angeles Crummett, "Rural Women and Industrial Home Work in Latin America: Research Review and Agenda," World Employment Programme Research Working Paper

(Geneva: International Labor Office, 1988).

13 Benería and Feldman, *Unequal Burden*; Benería and Roldán, *The Crossroads of Class and Gender*.

14 For examples of this literature, see Gillian Pascall, *Social Policy: A Feminist Analysis* (London: Tavistock Publications, 1986); Anne Showstack Sassoon, ed., *Women and the State* (London: Hutchinson, 1987); see also the journal *Social Politics: International Studies in Gender, State and Society*; Rowbotham and Mitter, *Dignity and Daily Bread*; Rowbotham, *Homeworkers Worldwide*.

15 For more information on these organizations, see Kalima Rose, *Where Women Are Leaders: The SEWA Movement in India* (London: Zed Books, 1992); Marty Chen, "The Working Women's Forum: Organizing for Credit and Change," in *SEEDS: Supporting Women's Work in the Third World*, ed. Ann Leonard (New York: Feminist Press, 1989), pp. 51–72; and Leslie J. Calman, *Toward Empowerment: Women and Movement Politics in India* (Boulder, Colo.: Westview Press, 1992), ch. 7.

2 »

Sexual Divisions, Gender Constructions

The Historical Meaning of Homework in Western Europe and the United States

« *Eileen Boris*

When the subject is homeworkers, all fantasies are possible.
—Jeanne Bouvier, 1936

A SEAMSTRESS TURNED HOMEWORKER ADVOCATE AND LABOR STANDARDS enforcer, Jeanne Bouvier looked back at nearly thirty years of activism with great sadness. Even after a 1915 French law provided a minimum wage for garment homeworkers, the debate over homework still pivoted around its impact on home and family.[1] Beginning in the late nineteenth century in leading industrial nations—France, Germany, Great Britain, and the United States—homework occupied the terrain on which questions of national strength, state intervention in the labor contract, and married women's wage earning became subjects of political struggle. Homeworkers were the objects of journalists' exposés and government investigations into the evil of sweated labor: production under conditions of poor sanitation, long working hours, speed-up, and low wages. They became the subject of reform efforts by middle-class women, religious organizations, and some employers and trade unionists. Although they served as living demonstrations of the negative impact of industrialization on the family, homeworkers were invisible: Not only were they hidden workers, whose labor occurred behind closed doors, but their voices and needs only rarely emerged in outsider constructions of the homework problem. Because of the persistent sexual division of labor in Western Europe and the

United States, the homework system depended on gender conventions, on attitudes toward home and married women that rationalized the existence of homework but also came to be used as reasons to justify its abolition. Through such constructions of homework, we witness the ideological separation of mother from worker and home from work, despite their actual connection in the homework system.

This chapter considers the history of homework from the late eighteenth century through World War I in terms of overall economic development and in relation to evolving understandings of gender: womanhood, manhood, and the proper relation between the two.[2] Indeed, women's need to engage in such labor highly correlated with men's relation to wage labor and responsibility within the family. Married women with small children whose husbands failed to earn adequate incomes (through unemployment, disability, or low wages) composed the majority of homeworkers in the industrializing nations this essay focuses on: the United States, Great Britain, France, and Germany. Even though the pace and contours of industrialization differed in these nations, homework, homeworkers, and the reformer constructed homework problem offer striking similarities that suggest shared gender conventions.

Rather than a residual form of production, home labor in industries that produced garments, textiles, cigars, artificial flowers, and numerous other consumer goods was integral to the industrial revolution in the core capitalist economies. Cottage industry or manufacturing in the home—sometimes referred to as protoindustrialization—had a shorter life in the United States than in Western Europe, and domestic industry persisted longer in Germany and France than in Great Britain. Employers' putting out of materials for manufacturing in home workshops often preceded factory production in Europe, in contrast to the United States, but home production also continued after the establishment of factories, as in the hosiery industry of Leicester. Though subject to uneven development, depending on the industry and region, homework generally grew in a symbiotic relation to the factory system in all these nation-states. Homeworkers were "invisible threads," as Karl Marx called them, "an outside department of the factory, the manufactory, or the warehouse."[3] They were wage earners, proletarians. Emerging along with capitalism in the countryside, homework characterized key consumer industries of nineteenth-century metropolitan industrialization.[4]

In some places, homework remained rural. In Germany and Sweden, for example, a close connection between domestic industry and agriculture persisted into the twentieth century as farm families supplemented their income through outwork during the winter months. After all, both agriculture and many homework industries were seasonal.[5] Weaving had provided additional income for peasant cottagers since at least the late sixteenth century, when household production entered the capitalist marketplace. Many guildsmen considered such labor dishonorable because it was pursued by untrained women within the household. Jean H. Quataert tells us that "artisanal practice identified productive work as properly male and domestic activities in households as properly female." This working-class linkage of homework with women's housework belied the existence of the family labor force prevalent in early domestic industry even as it anticipated the gendered ideology behind garment homework in the nineteenth and twentieth centuries. Household production continued in France throughout the nineteenth century; as Louise Tilly notes, it "was preserved in some proletarianized production" even among families who owned their looms.[6]

By 1900, garment homework in urban areas became the most prevalent form of home production. Sweated home industry mushroomed in turn of the century Paris.[7] The last third of the nineteenth century saw Berlin's "burgeoning apparel trade...transformed...into a widespread urban home industry," dependent on "the cheap labor of working-class wives and daughters."[8] London, New York, and other major Anglo-American cities housed extensive garment homeworking in growing tenement districts, areas where immigrants lived.[9]

In Britain as well as Germany and France, domestic industry became feminized, especially in textiles, clothing, and tobacco. As men increasingly entered "mechanized" factories, the subcontracting system brought homework to women in the garment industry and related trades such as embroidery, artificial flowers, and shoemaking. Men left the textile home industry in Germany much more quickly than women did; by 1907, women were the majority of the remaining textile home workers. In 1900, about half of French women wage earners labored at home.[10] One study estimates that in 1901 more than 70 percent of clothing homeworkers in London were women; in 1911, more than a quarter of married women there earned wages.[11]

Homework moved from part of a family labor system—as in shoemaking, where the wife sewed uppers for her husband—to a wage-labor system in which women assembled goods for men who were usually not their kin. In the United States, outwork represented a strategy first for rural women, daughters and mothers, to earn cash and later for immigrant mothers in urban tenement house districts to make ends meet. As early as the late eighteenth century, hundreds of women and children in Boston, New York, and Philadelphia worked in their homes setting teeth into carding combs, spinning and weaving, and making shoes. Although their rural counterparts wove intermittently, urban shirtmakers sewed "from sunrise till 10 or 11 o'clock at night," as investigator Helen Sumner noted in 1911. Initially they made entire shirts, but soon they merely put on sleeves or finished garments as the labor process became more divided. By midcentury, merchant tailors were sending work to home seamstresses in Britain, France, and Germany as well as the United States. An oversupply of labor in London made that city a center of sweated industry in which "slop-work," or the cheap ready-made trades, drew on female out-workers to undercut skilled male labor. Industrial homework and working-class consumption of manufactured goods were born together.[12]

As Shelley Pennington and Belinda Westover have shown, four factors determined women's homework in mid-nineteenth-century Britain. Low male wages, a pattern of casual seasonal labor for men, lack of alternative employment for women, and an oversupply of female labor characterized areas with extensive homework. London, the chain- and nail-making region of Cradley Heath, and Nottingham all harbored extensive homework. Leeds, a center of the clothing industry, had less homework, but even there the logic of production—such as floorspace, cost factors, and efficiencies of divided labor—pushed some processes into homes.[13]

Mechanization did not necessarily impede outwork; for example, the Singer sewing machine, with installment purchase plans, offered more women the opportunity to take work in because they no longer had to rely on hand-sewing skills. Increased manufacturing generated the home-based paper box industry. Technology, then, tended to alter rather than displace homework. The cost and supply of labor remained deciding factors: Homeworkers were cheaper handworkers who could also draw on the labor of children and other unpaid helpers whose combined efforts on piecework increased the daily wage. Still Quataert suggests that technology or its lack alone cannot account for homework: Berlin clothing factories were quick to mechanize. Rather, she reminds us, "normative expectations about women's proper work and family responsibilities helped shape the industry's final decentralized form as much as cost factors in an expensive urban climate."[14]

The development of the ready-made market further transformed tailoring, the major homework industry, by the late nineteenth century. In France, large department stores had encouraged the subcontracting system since midcentury. In the United States, the Civil War initiated the same kind of shift as the government relied on contractors to manufacture uniforms, leading to increased standardization of sizes. Manufacturers crafted the contract system to protect themselves from a fluctuating economy. Irregularity and seasonality came to characterize the entire industry, with rush seasons followed by fallow periods of up to three or four months a year. By 1892, only about half of all goods were made up in the contractor's own shop; at least a quarter of the half sent out went to tenement workshops where living and manufacturing mingled; and another quarter came to tenement homemakers, usually women. By that year, French statistics show that homeworkers comprised a fifth of all women in the labor force. Although domestic industry declined in Germany during the turn of the century, homework increased in urban areas, especially in the clothing trades that women dominated.[15]

In the late nineteenth century, protective labor legislation—maximum hours, minimum wages, and workplace restrictions, usually for women, along with limits on child labor—apparently increased the extent of homework. None of the early factory acts covered home-based workers. Thus, employers sought to maneuver around restrictive laws by sending work home after hours with factory employees or by closing down and reopening as homework distributors. Lace and hosiery manufacturers in Britain, for example, evaded the 1867 Factory Act through homework.[16] By granting immunity to the *atelier de famille*, French legislation designed to "protect" women workers actually multiplied the number of "small, allegedly 'family' workshops," or sweatshops, as Marilyn J. Boxer has shown. From 1896 to 1901, French garment workers at home grew from 51.8 to 58.6 percent.[17] In the United States, child labor laws, for example in New York, also failed to include homework. An 1891 act that prohibited child labor in German factories pushed young workers into the home. Indeed, Germany's extensive social insurance system excluded homeworkers because only those who performed labor classified as work under the 1869 industrial code qualified. In this system of classification, the state considered needlework, spinning, and knitting within the home as housework or female domestic arts rather than real work, like labor performed outside the home and associated with men. Moreover, the law did not classify family members who assisted self-employed male weavers as workers.[18] In Britain, such family members were exempt from the Factory and Workshop Consolidation Act of 1878, an omission that was not rectified until the first decade of the twentieth century. The Sanitary Commission on Sweating and the Homework System explained that "we think it desirable to interfere as little as possible with the habits and arrangements of families."[19] The initial Dutch protective laws of 1874 had similar consequences: removed to private houses, child labor and long hours for women would supposedly be protected because they were located in the realm of private life, but in fact they stood removed from state interference.[20]

Notions of privacy particularly inhibited state intervention into the family and the home in the United States. National Consumers' League executive Florence Kelley, a staunch crusader against homework, complained in 1905 that "parental exploitation of young children within the home did not technically constitute cruelty in the judicial sense." The separation of home from work, private from public, protected "the selfishness of parents and employ-ers." Since the 1880s, when the highest state court struck down New York's pioneer prohibition of tenement house cigarmaking, courts had upheld a man's freedom within his own home. Such a notion of privacy, added to the courts' newly minted right to contract, meant that any legislation on homework could merely regulate health and sanitary conditions within the home, not limit fam-ily members from performing waged labor there.[21] French reformers would forge a similar argument: "Hygienic and eugenic considerations overrode the 'inviolability of the home.'" Privacy, however, was not only a consideration of law; homeworkers themselves resented state invasion of their abodes. In 1877, speaking before a trade union conference, Mrs. Mason of the Leicestershire Seamers' and Stitchers' Society, a homeworkers' union founded by the British Women's Trade Union League, rejected coverage of homeworkers under the Factory and Workshop Act because "there were times when it was hardly desirable to have their houses inspected."[22]

The idea of the home as a separate sphere from the world of work, one the realm of woman and the other the domain of man, shaped the meaning of the sexual division of labor. As Quataert has pointed out, "for both artisans and Romantics, housewife was the adult woman's true 'occupation.'" Women of the middle and upper classes became defined as mothers; their economic con-tribution to the family became invisible as domestic labor lost its value. The idealization of motherhood further separated nurturing and dependent care from work. Thus wage labor became identified with the ideal worker as a man, because women—no matter what their actual life situation—were to care for children and maintain households.[23]

Certainly working-class conceptions of respectability merged with, even as they were influenced by, such bourgeois understandings of the home as woman's proper place. The daughter of a Colchester homeworker remem-bered: "They seemed to think if a woman worked after marriage ... it was something to be ashamed of. You were looked down on. You could do it at home and they didn't take too much notice of it." Another woman explained: "They used to cry shame on them in them days when they were married if they went out to work. They used to say your husband should keep you." Women's work in factories stigmatized men, announcing a man's inability to support his family and thus destroying his respectability. In Victorian and Edwardian England, "respectable" widows and lower-middle-class women and girls took sewing in; some even sent their servants to fetch the work. Wives of clerks and tradesmen could maintain family status through the clandestine nature of homework. Similarly, midcentury daughters of middle- and lower-middle-class Prussian families attended sewing schools where the boundaries between factory, school, and apprenticeship faded. These women were preparing for taking in garment work.[24]

Home labor had a redeeming feature missing from women's other industrial pursuits: its location. In 1803, Berlin tailors declared: "Married women must be maintained by their husbands, know housekeeping, and care for and educate their children." The unmarried could become domestic servants or "engage in other feminine occupations outside regular manufacture." A century later, other German opponents of women's industrial labor claimed that "in the confines of the home, the woman is influenced by tradition. Entrance into the labor force brings about drastic social change." But factory labor also undermined women's health, which meant, as one delegate to the Workers' Congress of 1876 in Paris exclaimed, that "family life will soon disintegrate and indifference will replace affection in the household." This association of degeneration with women's factory labor echoed the words of socialist J. P. Proudhon, who contended that "the working-class family has been disorganized by the industrial regime," which turned father into a wage earner and tore mother away from "her domestic sphere of influence."[25]

"Idealization of the family workshop," with its evocation of a former "family-based corporate order," certainly entered into such French pronouncements. Republican politician Jules Simon asserted in 1861 that woman's nature and education determined that she should not labor, but "men's wages being insufficient, ...then she can work at home; that is all society can allow." Twenty years later, a delegate to the Fourth National Workers' Congress argued that "if the woman must work, let her look for an occupation that will not remove her from the home. She will earn a little less maybe, but there will be nevertheless great benefits to be gained from her remaining at home." Social conservatives agreed, "dream[ing] of rebuilding homework on the ruins of the modern factory" and ending the separation between home and work wrought by mechanized production. Employers took up this call. In France, knitting-machine companies promised social stability with the purchase or lease of their machines. One historian has summarized their appeal: "The grandmother could look after the children, the mother could consecrate her free time to taking charge of her family, and even the young daughter could lend a helping hand thus avoiding the promiscuities which were thought inherent in factory life." But precisely because homework had become "a mere annex to the factory, the old conception of domestic industry, combined with family life," no longer could guide those who sought to curb employer abuses of the system. This transformation in the nature of home-based labor justified "interference" in the home in the minds of German reformers who lobbied for control of "Hausindustrie" and "Heimarbeit" in the early years of the new century.[26]

Catholic intellectuals, who defended the patriarchal family, initially embraced homework. Even after recognizing the evils of the homework system, Catholic reformers would seek to improve its conditions rather than abolish the practice. At the turn of the century, one leader in the Association Catholique explained: "Take away competition and secure legal protection for the workers; things will then change and home industry will once again succeed in bringing about a reconstitution of the family." But many others were joining Catholic corporatist Count Albert de Mun, who became convinced that homework, rather than factory labor, destabilized the family.[27]

In contrast to the French, who saw homework as a solution for disrupted families, skilled workers in the United States never argued that homework was a better option than factory labor for women. Employers, however, justified their use of the homework system in those terms, claiming that they could not find women who would work outside the home. Male artisans feared competition from homeworkers as much as from cheaper female labor in factories. Even though men and women rarely did the same work, homeworkers produced substitute consumer items whose lesser cost could lead to the unemployment of those who manufactured a higher-priced good. Homework threatened working-class men's perceived right to serve as breadwinners who earned a family wage. Samuel Gompers of the Cigarmakers' International Union, who was later president of the American Federation of Labor (AFL), warned in 1877 that employers who introduced tenement house competition against working-class men "would be responsible for any violent action that might be taken to protect their wives and children, and provide them with bread."[28] Male trade unionists in Britain similarly fought homework, calling for the abolition of a system that reduced wages, worsened working conditions, and impeded unionization. They too believed, as Henry Broadhurst told the 1877 meeting of the Trade Union Congress, that "it was their duty as men and husbands to use their utmost efforts to bring about a condition of things where their wives should be in their proper sphere at home, seeing after the house and family instead of being dragged into competition against the great and strong men of the world."[29]

But it was precisely because men could not earn a family wage that women turned to homework. Social investigators defined homeworkers in terms of their relation to men: as single or widowed; deserted or separated; wives with husbands permanently unemployed, unable to earn adequate wages, or disabled or ill. In addition, reformers usually saw homeworkers in relation to children, who confined many women to homework. In this instance, social categories matched demographic data. For example, most Nottingham married women homeworkers were lace clippers. Their husbands, many of whom were in the building trades, could obtain only intermittent labor. The male bread-winners of homeworking families in West Ham, London, in 1907 were also subject to irregular employment. Husbands of home finishers in major U.S. garment cities in 1911 earned less than those of shop finishers. The home-workers contributed a quarter of family income. In Germany, it was said of such a working-class wife that "she at the very least pays the rent." Since all working-class families suffered from unemployment, seasonal work, illnesses, and inadequate wages, what pushed some families to homework?[30]

Employers organized particular industries to take advantage of the avail-able labor force of women with reproductive and other domestic responsibil-ities. Younger children were characteristic of homeworking families, and homework served as a strategy for many working-class women to earn a wage at a particular point in their life cycle. As one British homeworker explained, "If I go to the factory I must buy milk for my child. If I stay at home I can give it the breast, as I ought." A spokeswoman for the National Home Workers League testified before Parliament in 1908 that homework allowed women to combine family labor and wage earning. Without homework, they would have to pay for child care, laundry, and prepared foods. "If they stay at home they can do their own housework and their own shopping; and can better care for children. If work is slack there is housework and mending and other domestic chores to be done."[31] At the time, there were few nurseries, and those that did exist were usually run by charities or philanthropists whose understandings of childhood and home and whose religions and ethnicities often contrasted and clashed with those of working-class women. Skill apparently stood in an inverse relation to child care as a reason to work at home; among Parisian flowermak-ers, Boxer found that only the least skilled took in work because of their chil-dren; these women were also married to unskilled men to a greater extent than more accomplished craftswomen. More skilled flowermakers saw themselves as artisans practicing their craft in their home workshops rather than as moth-ers without choices for childcare.[32]

During the early twentieth century, for Italian women in urban centers of the United States, homework meant not the destruction of the home but the fulfill-ment of familial duties. A young factory worker admitted choosing artificial flower manufacture because "it is the Italian's trade; and then I thought that when I get married I can still keep it up at home." Another daughter brought home flowers to finish after factory hours to earn the funds to send her elder brother to medical school. "I often say to my mother that we treat my brother as if he were a king,—but I can't help it," she confessed.[33] Similarly, members of British working-class families knew that the mother "did tailoring" because "she had to keep us going." She was the one whose small earnings "feed us kids."[34]

These were resourceful and hardworking women who turned into victims in a reform discourse that portrayed homeworkers as pathetic drudges. The language of dirt, darkness, and disease informed reform campaigns. "Day after day the same round of unskilled work, the same journeys to and from the factory, and the same rush to fit in the work of the household, whenever time can be snatched from the industry which has stepped in to take the first place in the home," or so Clementina Black of the Women's Industrial Council described London homework in 1897. Black not only condemned the low wages of home industry but also castigated "this constant grind and uncertainty, this want of pride in their work, and this sacrifice of all home comfort and orderliness to the industry." This view ignored the pride of the skilled embroiderer who was thrilled because "you couldn't tell a hand had touched [the socks] when she'd done." Of course, there were also shoe machinists who recalled their low rates as "absolute slavery,"[35] but it was reformers, not the women workers themselves, who equated homework with "the wreck of the home," or with "squalid and unwholesome surroundings." French Consumers' League director Henriette Brunhes chided defenders of homework: "Do you call this a 'family'?...a poor hovel, turned into a shop, where human beings are packed for fifteen to sixteen hours at a time?" Compared to other forms of employment, she described homework as "more unhealthy, more extended, more underpaid, more immoral, more resistant to all reform and all surveillance, more contrary to all social progress by means of group organization."[36]

Homework negated the notion of a proper home held by such self-appointed protectors of wage-earning mothers. "'Home and mother!' Our grim system forces hundreds of thousands to lose the meanings of these sweet old words," muckraking poet Edwin Markham declared in 1907. The home was a place of rest, the opposite of the factory or workplace. Anti-sweating leader Sir Charles Dilke explained: "The home becomes the grinding shop. Factory slavery finds a refuge even in a hard home. 'Home' slavery has none." Future British prime minister Ramsey MacDonald refused to "recognise the home as a proper place for work being done, whether you get 5d. per hour, or 5 farthings per hour, or nothing per hour." His wife, Margaret MacDonald, a leader in the Women's Industrial Council, considered licensing of homework (until industry could be reorganized) justified in order to maintain the health of the nation. "A woman's home duties are not only her own personal affair but they concern the welfare of the community. The State is interested not only that she should bear healthy children but also that she should have time to attend to their needs."[37] Such reformers believed that the long hours demanded by the low piece rates of homework interfered with a mother's larger social duty. Even before the British fear of losing imperial stature developed, French Republican feminists had associated depopulation and national power with women's familial roles; since homework undermined these roles, it became a scourge to the nation as well as to the bodies of its inhabitants.[38]

Many middle-class women reformers adhered to the belief that women belonged at home. Some told the British Trade Union Congress that "the question of the employment of women and their industrial organisation bore upon the well-being of their husbands, their children and their homes." They agreed that "women were best in their own homes...but unfortunately, there were women who were not able to remain in their own homes and who were compelled to work."[39] Social feminists in the United States defended the rights of working women to a living wage but preferred to see mothers remain at home. Their feminism of difference tended to reject paid labor in the name of improving the lives of women strained to the "limit of human endurance" by "bearing, nursing and taking care of...children and at the very same time and place trying to earn a wage." Homework generated the worse consequences, these women believed. Because women's domestic and maternal responsibilities went unquestioned, policy options became limited: Do away with homework and eliminate the necessity of mothers' wage earning either through a family wage paid to the male household head or, if no male head was present, pay a pension to the mother. Licensing of homeworkers became the first step to end homework.[40]

Focused on community needs, licensing was intended to protect the consumer from contaminated products. Women who organized consumer leagues in the United States and in France drew in particular on bourgeois women's responsibility as shoppers to shape a gendered political economy. Dominant gender constructions designated women as the caretakers of their sex and dependent persons: Privileged women entered the public sphere through performing such duties among the less fortunate. The consumer leagues stressed the connection between "women who work" and "women who spend." The wise consumer would benefit not only her family but all women through indirect philanthropy. In France, La Ligue Sociale d'Acheteurs mobilized to fight "against cheapness," to educate consumers "that to purchase ready-to-wear garments, without knowing either the origin or the cost of production, is equal to outwardly favoring the exploitation of the homeworkers, and that in some instances you are also purchasing tuberculosis, diphtheria, measles, or scarlet fever." Rather than questioning gender conventions, the leagues used them to improve the conditions of less fortunate "sisters." Self-protection, fear of the disease that might lurk in clothes made in improper homes, joined reason, sentiment, and guilt to motivate the ethical shopper.[41]

Licensing programs also accepted the existing sexual division of labor by defining the homeworker as a mother seeking to improve her workplace but not her wages. Licensing was the prevalent form of intervention in the United States, though by 1912 the National Consumers' League was championing the minimum wage to curtail homework. The British Trade Board Act of 1909 (which modeled such boards on Australian wage boards) presented the minimum wage as an alternative solution to the homework problem. So had the first international congress of consumers leagues, which met in Geneva in 1908. In theory applicable to both sexes, trade boards in fact covered sweated industries in which women predominated. With minimum wages, the homeworker became recognized as a worker and not merely a working mother. British Women's Trade Union League secretary Mary MacArthur, a prominent proponent of the trade boards and mass unionization of women (including homeworkers), defended "the right of women to work": "Man has never objected to women working," she declared at the 1909 Trade Union Congress. "It is her wage-earning which distresses the masculine mind."[42]

Women proponents of minimum wages for women often equated *minimum* with living wages, and some women workers saw minimum wages as compatible with homework.[43] A founder of the flowermaking cooperative L'Oeuvre des Artisans Parisiennes justified homework because "there are many women who have good reasons to stay at home and who must however earn a living," and they deserved "a just, daily minimum living wage." Homeworkers organized by the Catholic Syndicat des Ouvrières de l'Aiguille à Domicile reacted more cautiously to the idea of the minimum wage. Believing that no general minimum was possible, they also feared too high a wage would force "mothers of working families...to abandon their families to seek employment in the workshop (and the young woman will find it simpler to abstain from having children)."[44]

Trade unionists generally saw the minimum wage as based on women's needs, which were fewer than men's. After all, women belonged in the home, with the family, taking care of men. The minimum, then, was precisely that. Socialist and social democratic parties all over Europe passed resolutions condemning homework. The 1904 Berlin Congress called for gradual abolition of homework rather than the minimum wage: "In the modern mode of production, home industry brings the most harmful economic and physical consequences to the workers.... Legislation should protect the workers and the public." Opponents of homework believed that it undercut the wages of other workers. Socialist feminists agreed on abolition, although their reasons differed from those of their male colleagues. Stephanie Bouvard of the Chambre Syndicale des Ouvrières Fleuristes, Plumassières et Métiers Similaires claimed:

"The work of the woman at home is an obstacle to her emancipation; instead of coming to our meetings, enriching and educating herself, the woman remains at home.... If we encourage woman's work in the home, we lose an important means of emancipation." Another group declared that "The 'Angel in the House' ideal no longer exists! ...Our feminism consists above all in elevating the woman, to put her in her true place in society, to make her equal to man in every respect." Homework stymied the accomplishment of that goal.[45]

In France, homeworker unions as well as such "revolutionary feminists" argued for a law that covered both sexes and all home industry; the 1915 minimum wage act applied only to women in the garment trade. Its definition constructed the homeworker as an inferior worker by defining the minimum wage as "not...less than the average wages payable by the hour or the day to an unskilled worker in the locality in question." Unlike factory legislation, this act gave inspectors no power to enter the home workplace, a limit to effective regulation that reflected a belief in the privacy of the home held by all sectors of society, including homeworkers.[46] The German act of 1911, in contrast, included persons working at home alone or with family members and also those laboring "in a non-factory affiliated workshop." Employers had to keep lists of their employees ready for state use, and contractors had to provide information on wages and hours. But employers continued to set wages, and much of the act never went into effect because of World War I.[47] In the United States, as has been noted, state laws allowed inspectors to check the sanitary condition of tenements, but failed to control wage rates. Only during World War I did the federal government restrict homework by prohibiting home manufacture of army uniforms. In this case, the working mothers of the tenements were excluded from the population that should benefit from the industrial democracy heralded by the Wilson administration. Instead, Wilsonians viewed these women as obstacles to decent wages and working conditions for garment workers in the shops; they were defined as mothers rather than workers.[48]

The British trade boards promised a different outcome. In 1910, the first four boards covered chain making, lace and net making, paperbox making, and "bespoke" tailoring, all industries in which women suffered from low wages and long hours. As Sheila Rowbotham has pointed out, such state intervention was not necessarily an alternative to self-organization of homeworkers. "Both feminists, who stressed the importance of suffrage, and women trade unionists, put various degrees of emphasis upon the *combination* of mobilisation of casual women workers and state intervention," as Rowbotham notes. For example, Mary MacArthur viewed the low wages of homeworkers as part of a problem facing all women wage earners. In Cradley Heath, where a history of organization existed among a fixed population of home-based women chain makers (men worked in factories in the sexual division of labor within this trade), the National Federation of Women Workers helped mobilize the women, whom employers locked out of work after the trade board introduced its minimum wage. These women won an increased wage set by the board and encouraged other nearby women in the Birmingham area to organize. But the political economy in other trades left a more mixed legacy. Foreign competition led to low rates in both lace and box making. Lace making employed women in more desperate circumstances than the chainmakers because their men held more casualized jobs. Thus, the family economy of workers could shape the outcome of such conflicts as much as the organization of the industry. Although clothing workers improved their organization after the Trades Board Act, homeworkers hardly benefited because piece rates remained in the hands of employers and the board set differential rates based on sex.[49]

In legislating against homework, all of these countries tended to separate homeworkers from other workers. There were workers and women workers, the latter category distinguished from the former, which embedded within its apparent gender neutrality the expectation of the masculine.[50] In part this separation also reflected reform portraits of the homeworker as an inefficient producer and of homework as an outdated mode of production. Such a conception drew upon more generalized understandings of gender: Women were reproducers and consumers rather than producers.[51] Homeworking mothers were victims of exploitation whose wage labor got in the way of their real work—child care and household maintenance. As mothers rather than workers they needed protection, education, and aid. Other workers should receive the living wages that their families required, and if no wage earners were present, then the state should provide aid so that they could perform their duty as mothers of future citizens. These categories shaped the discussions of the ILO in the 1920s and 1930s, couched in terms of minimum wages and the general characteristics of sweated labor. As Elisabeth Prügl has shown, the international consensus groped toward an understanding of homeworkers as "mothers in peril," a justification for prohibition of such work. Homeworkers became nonworkers as labor standards increasingly referred to factories and other extra-domestic workplaces, disregarding those who labored at home.[52] This dichotomy—between mother and worker, home and workplace—built on existing sexual divisions of labor. It became embedded in labor standards law, where it continues to shape public discourse on home-based labor.

Notes

1   Jeanne Bouvier, *Mes memoires ou 59 années d'activité industrielle, sociale et intellectuelle d'une ouvrière*, as quoted in Marilyn J. Boxer, "Protective Legislation and Home Industry: The Marginalization of Women Workers in Late Nineteeth–Early Twentieth Century France," *Journal of Social History* 20 (Fall 1986): 64, n.31. See also Lorraine Coons, "'Neglected Sisters' of the Women's Movement: The Perception and Experience of Working Mothers in the Parisian Garment Industry, 1860–1915," *Journal of Women's History* 5 (Fall 1993): 56–59; and Coons, *Women Home Workers in the Parisian Garment Industry, 1860–1915* (New York: Garland Publishing, Inc., 1987).

2   Joan Wallach Scott, "Gender: A Useful Category of Historical Analysis," in *Gender and the Politics of History* (New York: Columbia University Press, 1988), pp. 28–50; and Judith Butler, *Gender Trouble: Feminism and the Subversion of Identity* (New York: Routledge, 1990).

3   Karl Marx, *Capital*, Volume 1 (New York: International Publishers, 1967), p. 461.

4   See Franklin F. Mendels, "Proto-Industrialization: The First Phase of the Industrialization Process," *Journal of Economic History* 32 (1972): 241–261; Christopher Clark, *The Roots of Rural Capitalism: Western Massachusetts, 1780–1860* (Ithaca, N.Y.: Cornell University Press, 1990); Barbara Franzoi, "'…with the wolf always at the door.…': Women's Work in Domestic Industry in Britain and Germany," in *Connecting Spheres: Women in the Western World, 1500 to the Present*, eds. Marilyn J. Boxer and Jean H. Quataert (New York: Oxford University Press, 1987), pp. 146–155; Jamie Faricellia Dangler, "Industrial Homework in the Modern World-Economy," *Contemporary Crises* 10 (1986): 259–264; and Nancy Grey Osterud, "Gender Divisions and the Organization of Work in the Leicester Hoisery Industry," in *Unequal Opportunities: Women's Employment in England, 1800–1918*, ed. Angela V. John (Oxford: Basil Blackwell, 1986), pp. 45–68. See also, Selma Leydesdorff, "Hidden Work: Outwork in Dutch Industrialisation," in *Retrieving Women's History: Changing Perceptions of the Role of Women in Politics and Society*, ed. S. Jay Kleinberg (Oxford: Berg/UNESCO, 1988), pp. 166–169, for a description of how the factory system created a form of homework distingushed from domestic industry.

5   Ruth Shallcross, *Industrial Homework: An Analysis of Homework Regulation Here and Abroad* (New York: Industrial Affairs, 1939), p. 14.

6   Jean H. Quataert, "The Shaping of Women's Work in Manufacturing: Guilds, Households, and the State in Central Europe, 1648–1870," *American Historical Review* 90 (December 1985): 1122–1148, esp. 1133–1135; Louise A. Tilly, "Paths of Proletarianization: Organization of Production, Sexual Division of Labor, and Women's Collective Action," *Signs: A Journal of Women in Culture and Society* 7 (Winter 1981): 402–406.

7   Coons, *Women Home Workers*; Boxer, "Protective Legislation and Home Industry," pp. 45, 49.

8   Barbara Franzoi, *At the Very Least She Pays the Rent: Women and German*

Industrialization, 1871–1914 (Westport, Conn.: Greenwood Press, 1985); Quataert, "The Shaping of Women's Work in Manufacturing," pp. 1143–1144.

9   James A. Schmiechen, *Sweated Industries and Sweated Labor: The London Clothing Trades, 1860–1914* (Urbana: University of Illinois Press, 1984); Eileen Boris, *Home to Work: Motherhood and the Politics of Industrial Homework in the United States* (New York: Cambridge University Press, 1994), pp. 51–52.

10   For overall trends in Britain, France, and Germany and for French statistics, see Laura Levine Frader, "'Women in the Industrial Capitalist Economy," in *Becoming Visible: Women in European History*, 2nd ed., eds. Renate Bridenthal, Claudia Koonz, and Susan Stuard (Boston: Houghton Mifflin Co, 1987), p. 324; for Germany, see Franzoi, "'….with the wolf always at the door….'," p. 149; Franzoi, *At the Very Least She Pays the Rent*, pp. 127–129.

11   Schmiechen, *Sweated Industries and Sweated Labor*, pp. 66–71. Married women were not a separate category in English census tabulations until 1911.

12   See Mary Blewett, *Men, Women, and Work: Class, Gender, and Protest in the New England Shoe Industry, 1790–1910* (Urbana: University of Illinois Press, 1988); Thomas Dublin, "Rural Putting-Out Work in Early Nineteenth-Century New England: Women and the Transition to Capitalism in the Countryside," *New England Quarterly* 64 (1991): 531–573; Helen Sumner, "History of Women in Industry in the United States," *Report on the Condition of Women and Children Wage Earners in the United States* v. 9, (Washington, D.C.: Government Printing Office [GPO], 1911), pp. 123–133; Edith Abbott, *Women in Industry: A Study in American Economic History* (New York: D. Appleton and Co., 1910), pp. 37–38, 40–41; Sally Alexander, "Women's Work in Nineteenth-Century London: A Study of the Years 1820–50," in *The Rights and Wrongs of Women*, eds. Juliet Mitchell and Ann Oakley (New York: Penguin, 1976), pp. 80–83, 97–110; and Shelley Pennington and Belinda Westover, *A Hidden Workforce: Homeworkers in England, 1850–1985* (London: Macmillan, 1989), pp. 39–40.

13   Pennington and Westover, *A Hidden Workforce*, pp. 30–50. See also, Jenny Morris, *Women Workers and the Sweated Trades: The Origins of Minimum Wage Legislation* (Aldershot, England: Gower, 1986), pp. 37–38; and Morris, "The Characteristics of Sweating: The Late Nineteenth Century London and Leeds Tailoring Trade," in *Unequal Opportunities*, pp. 95–112.

14   Pennington and Westover, *A Hidden Workforce*, pp. 33–41; Quataert, "The Shaping of Women's Work in Manufacturing," pp. 1144–1145.

15   See Coons, "'Neglected Sisters' of the Women's Movement," pp. 54–55; Mabel Hurd Willett, "The Employment of Women in the Clothing Trades," *Columbia University Studies in the Social Sciences* (New York: Columbia University Press, 1902); David Montgomery, *The Fall of the House of Labor: The Workplace, the State, and American Labor Activism, 1865–1925* (New York: Cambridge University Press, 1987), pp. 116–123; "Men's Ready-Made Clothing," *Report on the Conditions of Women and Children in Industry*, vol. 2 (Washington, D.C.: GPO, 1911), pp. 413–423; Franzoi, *At the Very Least She Pays the Rent*, p. 129.

16 Pennington and Westover, *A Hidden Workforce*, pp. 37, 39; Sonya Rose, *Limited Livelihoods: Gender and Class in Nineteenth-Century England* (Berkeley: University of California Press, 1992), pp. 74–75; Franzoi, *At the Very Least She Pays the Rent*, pp. 73–74, 76–77.

17 Boxer, "Protective Leislation and Home Industry," pp. 46–47; Mary Lynn Stewart, *Women, Work and the French State: Labour Protection and Social Patriarchy, 1879–1919* (Montreal: McGill-Queen's University Press, 1989), p. 69.

18 Boris, *Home to Work*, p. 116; Quataert, "The Shaping of Women's Work in Manufacturing," p. 1146; Jean H. Quataert, "Women's Work and the Early Welfare State in Germany: Legislators, Bureaucrats, and Clients Before the First World War," in *Mothers of a New World: Maternalist Politics and the Origins of Welfare States*, eds. Seth Koven and Sonya Michel (New York: Routledge, 1993), pp. 175–182.

19 Morris, *Women Workers and the Sweated Trades*, p. 173.

20 Leydesdorff, "Hidden Work," pp. 174–175.

21 Late nineteenth-century jurists in the United States found in the fourteenth amendment a "right to contract" that made it difficult to enact regulatory legislation that would interfere with the labor contract between corporations and individual adult male workers, both of whom the law recognized as people who could not have their freedom interfered with without due process. Florence Kelley, *Some Ethical Gains Through Legislation* (New York: Macmillan Company, 1905), p. 7; on New York's prohibition and consequent developments, see Boris, *Home to Work*, pp. 21–47.

22 Stewart, *Women, Work, and the French State*, p. 69; Mrs. Mason quoted in Shelia Rowbotham, "Strategies Against Sweated Work in Britain, 1820–1920," in *Dignity and Daily Bread: New Forms of Economic Organizing among Poor Women in the Third World and the First* (London: Routledge, 1994), pp. 166–167.

23 Quataert, "The Shaping of Women's Work in Manufacturing," pp. 1138–1139; see also Jeanne Boydston, *Home and Work: Housework, Wages, and the Ideology of Labor in the Early Republic* (New York: Oxford University Press, 1990).

24 Rose, *Limited Livelihoods*, p. 99; homeworkers quoted in Pennington and Westover, *A Hidden Workforce*, pp. 12, 18–22; Quataert, "The Shaping of Women's Work in Manufacturing," pp. 1135–1143.

25 Berlin tailors quoted in Quataert, "The Shaping of Women's Work in Manufacturing," p. 1134; German opponents quoted in Franzoi, *At the Very Least She Pays the Rent*, p. 18; French delegate quoted in Coons, "'Neglected Sisters' of the Women's Movement," p. 53; for Proudhon, see Coons, *Women Home Workers*, pp. 16–18.

26 Boxer, "Protective Legislation and Home Industry," pp. 48–49; Jules Simon quoted in Coons, *Women Home Workers*, pp. 19, 126–127; Fourth Workers' Conference quoted in Coons, "'Neglected Sisters' of the Women's Movement," p. 53; social conservatives quoted in Marilyn J. Boxer, "Women in Industrial Homework: The Flowermakers of Paris in the Belle Epoque," *French Historical*

almonds, which she didn't enjoy as much. All decisions regarding this widow's children—their education, their marriages, her son's career—were made by her husband's older brother. She observed strict purdah and was fearful of upsetting her brother-in-law. Because she was not his wife, she didn't have the opportunity to wait for "the right time" to discuss things with him; instead, she had no recourse but to listen to him.

Poverty and illiteracy also serve as constraints on women's greater participation in the economy. There are limited educational opportunities. There are many elementary schools for girls within the Walled City, such as the free school built by former prime minister Nawaz Sharif near Sheranwala Gate, but there are no secondary girls' schools. Many women told me they would have liked to have studied further but were unable to travel alone to a high school outside the city, and no male in their family was available to accompany them. Although there are many private and public sewing schools, there is no technical school for girls within the Walled City where they can learn industry-related skills.

Women often told me that social values are the most powerful constraint on women's economic activities. It is not only a question of a woman leaving her kucha and thereby bringing her morality into question, but the larger issue of a woman earning an income (or preparing to do so) and feeding the men in her family from that income. Women are not opposed to doing such a thing; they are just opposed to other people knowing about it. One woman astutely observed, "People think badly if a woman works at all. Whether she works as a lady doctor, or a teacher, people still say that her mother and father eat from her labor. The point is that whatever kind of work a girl does, if she has to walk outside to do it, it doesn't look good for the family. A girl can work inside of her home, and no one knows." Norms and values associated with the gendered division of space in the Walled City, however, are under severe strain in poor households, compelling women to work surreptitiously. Conditions of high density give rise to the fear that others in Walled City neighborhoods will track women's movements and activities; this fear may prevent teenaged girls from traveling to schools and limit the expansion of women's economic activities, but it does not prevent women from working or studying, given economic and social necessity.

Promoting Women's Empowerment in Home-Based Work

It is not enough simply to declare that women living in the Walled City either are working at low-paying jobs or would like to work but cannot find employment. Given this reality as well as the existing constraints on their working outside their homes, their limited education, and lack of financial resources, what kinds of possibilities can we envision that might increase the likelihood that those seeking gainful employment will find it?

Many of the women with whom I spoke had visions of what might be changed in their lives to facilitate their empowerment. For example, the establishment of a sewing cooperative network would bring them greater power. Many of the women already can sew, and ample opportunities exist to learn for those who cannot. With such a network, women could determine what they would sew and be able to obtain start-up money for their ventures. Building on this beginning, the Ministry for Women's Development could help establish a central cooperative/clearinghouse that could draw on the existing and varied expertise of women living in the Walled City. The clearinghouse could keep lists of skills that women have and list unskilled women who are willing to do some sort of cottage labor in their homes. Businesses could be given incentives such as import tax credits for providing raw materials to the cooperative and marketing the finished goods. Under such a system, what the women do and the environment in which it is done would not actually differ from the present situation. However, because they are unable to go to the bazaar and sell their goods directly to shopkeepers (given the social norms and values discussed earlier), such a clearinghouse network would enable them to enjoy steady work. Additionally, they would not live under the threat of having work arbitrarily withheld from them, and they would earn far more than they currently do when middlemen control the entire process.

We should recall Barbara Rogers's caution that cooperatives should emphasize the manufacture of goods whose economic importance to the larger economy is popularly recognized—in this case, clothes and household necessities—and should shy away from craft items and other goods made for tourist and overseas specialty markets, which sustain the invisibility of women's labor by perpetuating the idea that women do such work in their "free time."[11] This emphasis is particularly important in working-class areas such as the Walled City of Lahore, where the invisibility of female labor perpetuates the myth that women need not work and in turn further limits their employment options. The recognition of women's productive labor will inevitably open up additional political, economic, and social opportunities for women.

A second kind of suggestion emerged around creating a small-loan program for enterprising women who already are trained in some field and would like to start their own businesses. A training program covering such issues as small-business management, taxes, and marketing might be attached to the program. For example, the hairdresser who earns merely three dollars per week dreams of the day she might open her own shop. The cloth trader could make more profit if she could make her purchases in larger bulk, but that also takes an initial capital investment. A sickly widow who embroiders shirts on order feels she could earn more if she sells them directly, but she needs money to purchase the cloth and thread to get started. Being without a male wage earner is not unusual, and many women find themselves in this position at some stage of their lives. These women, like others, would prefer to earn for themselves rather than rely on their husbands' families for their support.

Such projects may also shed some light on the underlying contradictions that arise in the ongoing process of economic development and sociocultural transformation and on the kinds of alternatives that emerge as people living within the Walled City try to come to terms with these realities. Women and men are being forced, by the necessity of poverty and the changing structure of the extended family, to reallocate obligations, resulting in a redistribution of gender-based rights and power. Residents of the Walled City of Lahore, Pakistan, anchored in centuries-old traditions while being forced to confront the challenges of contemporary life, provide cogent examples of the renegotiation of gendered expectations.

An important result is that men are increasingly relinquishing some of the powerful control they have held over women and are also expecting women to take on different roles. We see an ongoing renegotiation of personal power and mobility within the family because of women's increased competencies. Men are also realizing that women do not need them as much as they did in the past and that it is now possible for women to be self-reliant. Needless to say, this change creates much confusion in a society where social norms still revolve around honor and respect, and there is a discernible increase in men's fears of what "uncontrolled," qualified women might do.

When we think of the work women do in the Walled City—sewing, embroidery, food preparation, stringing flowers—we are reminded of what life looks like outside on the streets. Both the cooperative and the small-loans program would only be a short-term solution to an immediate problem, but such ideas are a first step in recognizing the presence and importance of women in the work force. By empowering women's income-earning capacity, women are also empowered within the family, and this change is seminal to viable, long-term change.

Notes

This chapter is based on research elaborated in Anita M. Weiss, *Walls Within Walls: Life Histories of Working Women in the Old City of Lahore* (Boulder, CO: Westview Press, 1992).

1   A savory breakfast consisting of curried garbanzo beans and spiced leavened bread fresh from a *tandoor* oven.

2 A deep-fried dumpling, generally filled with a spicy potato mixture when sold in the Walled City of Lahore.

3 *Halwa* is fried, sweet semolina, to be eaten by hand with hot, deep-fried flat bread, *puri*, for breakfast.

4 A very hot and spicy meat curry, renowned as a Walled City specialty.

5 Fatima Mernissi, *Beyond the Veil: Male-Female Dynamics in a Modern Muslim Society*, rev. ed. (Bloomington: Indiana University Press, 1987), p. 148.

6 *Encyclopedia Britannica*, vol. 13, 14th ed. (London: Encyclopedia Britannica, 1929).

7 Apt comparisons, in particular, are Morocco and the old city of Cairo, Egypt. See Elizabeth Fernea, *A Street in Marrakech* (Garden City, N.Y.: Doubleday, 1975); Fatima Mernissi, *Doing Daily Battle* (New Brunswick, N.J.: Rutgers University Press, 1989); and Arlene Macleod, *Accommodating Protest* (New York: Columbia University Press, 1991).

8 Finance Division, Government of Pakistan, *Economic Survey, 1992–93* (Islamabad: Economic Adviser's Wing, July 1993), p. 111. These figures are estimates reported in the 1990–1991 Labor Force Survey.

9 The 1981 *District Census of Lahore* (Population Census Organisation, 1984), p. 74, reported that the Walled City's population was 190,000 in 1981. A World Bank/Lahore Development Authority (1980) study estimated that the Walled City's population would be 277,000 in 1986 (p. 22). More recent official figures are unavailable.

10 For details on methodology used in conducting both the random-sample survey of one hundred households and life history accounts of a representative group of women residents in the Walled City, see Weiss, *Walls Within Walls*, pp. xi–xiii.

11 For further elaboration on this argument, see Barbara Rogers, *The Domestication of Women: Discrimination in Developing Societies* (London: Tavistock Publications, 1980).

6 »

"Good Housewives"

Seamstresses in the Brazilian Garment Industry

« *Alice Rangel de Paiva Abreu and Bila Sorj*

ALL OVER THE WORLD, HOME-BASED WORK IS WOMEN'S WORK.[1] ALTHOUGH scholars and policy-makers generally acknowledge this fact, they usually present homeworking women as passive victims of entrepreneurial strategies. But to identify female home-based workers by their external links—that is, as economically subordinate to and dependent upon an employer or intermediary—takes into account only one set of the social relations that define their identity.[2] To assess women's behavior as productive workers, we need to explore the agency of the women who willingly undertake homework—their motives, their understandings, and the social relations sustaining their labor. Our research among homeworkers in the garment industry of Rio de Janeiro, Brazil,[3] illuminates both the gender subordination and the gendered strategies of women homeworkers. Thus, we emphasize the logic of the economic system less than that of the family subsystem. The view of workers as an abstract, exclusive category gives way to an approach that sees women workers in all of their multiple social roles.

Homeworkers are not only workers; they are also family members. Their attitudes toward waged labor, their consciousness as workers, and the conditions of their labor are closely linked with their role(s) in the family. In contrast to men, women in contemporary societies apparently find it difficult to construct an autonomous identity from roles and expectations situated within the world of the family.[4] A woman's individuality is constructed more frequently as that of a family member—someone's daughter, mother, or wife—than as a worker. This is certainly the case for homeworkers. An analysis of industrial homework must consider the gendered identities of these women, who closely experience the world of labor in connection with their domestic space. Homeworkers, however, are not passive victims in this space; they are active agents who strive to develop their potential within a context of economic and gender subordination.

The Garment Industry in Rio de Janeiro

A female labor market dominates the garment industry in Rio de Janeiro, as it does throughout the world. The women's fashion industry, which has developed over the past twenty years, consists of both small and medium-sized firms[5] and offers diverse possibilities for wage work. These opportunities range from a few highly skilled positions in big and medium-sized plants for patternmakers and qualified machinists with formal work contracts to much less formal jobs as machinists without contracts or young trainees at half pay. The last link in this heterogeneous chain is the homeworker, working for the small fashion firms. She is the invisible worker, uncounted in official statistics and not covered by specific labor or social legislation.[6]

Two practices usually determine homeworker wage contracts. Under the first, there is no signed work contract and no labor benefits: This situation is certainly more common. Some firms, however, treat homeworkers as "self-employed" workers who have to bear all social security–related costs. This arrangement is of course a convenient artifice to legalize an otherwise illegal situation. Homeworkers actually are wage laborers who should be entitled to all associated rights and guarantees. Brazilian labor courts have tended to grant equal employment rights to homeworking women who manage to prove that they had a regular work relationship with a firm.[7] However, few women seek such legal redress. Not only is it difficult to gain access to legal institutions, but women fear blacklisting by garment firms. Moreover, a feebly defined professional identity discourages homeworkers from turning to the legal system as a way of obtaining their rights.

Most women had a direct personal connection to the firms for which they worked.[8] Networks of friends, neighbors, and relatives formed the fabric of the labor market and played an important role in circulating job information, which would otherwise be unavailable to workers in a geographically scattered, low-profile, and highly informal market. Employers took full advantage of these networks. Very few (32 percent) of the homeworkers had been recruited by other means such as newspaper advertisements. In the recruitment of labor, then, we see an organization in which informal contacts within familial and community networks predominate.

Homework and Family Life

Garment homeworkers generally were older women with small children whose husbands or male partners lived with them at home.[9] The majority of the women were born in Rio, contrary to our expectation that there would be a high proportion of recent migrants. In the Brazilian context, these home-workers then belonged to a relatively stable social group. Their profile matched statistics for female labor force participation in the 1980 census. Participation rates in formal wage labor in urban areas decrease significantly among married women after their thirty-ninth year of age.[10] Greater difficulty in obtaining a formal wage contract after a certain age fails to explain, however, why some women turn specifically to homework when they could opt for other alternatives in the large Brazilian "informal" sector, such as street vending or paid domestic work.

Unlike many homeworkers throughout the world, these Brazilian women did not come from the very lowest social groups. One must remember that in Brazilian society there are still strict levels of social inequality, with low levels of absolute poverty. The homeworkers did belong to lower-working-class groups, but they lived in urbanized neighborhoods (not in *favelas*); their houses were made of brick (although they often lacked paint); and their husbands worked in the building industry, gas stations, urban transport, or lower urban services. They owned several household consumer goods such as a stove, a refrigerator, a television, or their own sewing machine. They lived in stable conjugal families with a higher family wage than the modal wage of the Brazilian labor force.

Many also belonged to Protestant sects that promote traditional gender roles. Of the hundred women interviewed, 25 percent professed the creed of one of the different Protestant sects active in Brazil. The rapid expansion of Evangelical religious groups and their activities in the poor neighborhoods of large Brazilian cities is a recent and significant phenomenon. The Institutional Evangelic Census of 1992 shows that in the area where most of our home-workers lived, the percentage of Evangelicals in the total population was 18.1 percent, while in the high-middle-class neighborhood it was only 6.6 percent.[11]

These homeworkers appeared to be strongly influenced by an ideology in which the position of woman was defined almost exclusively by her status as mother and wife. Homework apparently allowed a wage-earning activity to be exercised alongside the usual domestic obligations during a period in the life cycle in which such duties are especially heavy, with a husband and small children present. Seventy percent of the women gave their domestic situation as an explanation when asked why they had chosen homework. When asked to compare home-based work with factory work, 79 percent of the married women showed a strong preference for homework, compared with only 21 percent of single women. With identities so strongly defined by their roles as wives and mothers, these women became motivated to choose homework because it provided the possibility of reconciling income-earning activities with family demands.

The principles of gender construction established in families and society as a whole also operate when it comes to employers' hiring policies. Employers show a strong preference for middle-aged, married women with children. They associate the especially valued qualities of self-discipline, responsibility, seriousness, and punctuality with this category of women. Given lack of direct control or supervision of worker productivity, employers take advantage of the discipline imposed on women by the need to care for children and thus remain at home to earn money. Women's household and child-care duties firmly support the kind of behavior necessary to satisfy productive expectations of employers. Of course, this criterion alone is not enough to guarantee fulfillment of agreed-on production targets. Some firms use bonuses or prizes as a positive reinforcement or, alternatively, cut the piece rate if articles arrive past their deadline. Moreover, the same forces that discipline this labor force also can disrupt production because the immediate needs of children and pressure of home duties can interfere with wage-earning activities.

The ability to rely on a stable and well-known group of homeworkers is also important for the firm in order to minimize the risk of losing valuable raw material that must be entrusted to homeworkers. Middle-aged, married women with children seem to offer greater security than single women. They also have a narrower range of options on the employment market: Single women are more likely to take factory jobs should the opportunity arise. In the homework system, a certain type of employment matches the productive availability of a certain social group.

Talents, Skills, Work, and Employment

Most homeworkers had a lifelong relationship to the actual work of sewing and prided themselves on their skills as seamstresses. Several mentioned sewing as a vocation, recalling their commitment in learning how to sew and their first experiences with the sewing machine as a child. They were long-term homeworkers: 57 percent of the women interviewed had worked as homeworkers for more than ten years and 80 percent for more than six. This time span is in sharp contrast with their relation to their jobs, that is, to the firms for which they worked at the time of the interview: 76.3 percent had labored for their employers for less than three years. Such job instability strongly relates to perceptions of their own skill and the relationship between skill and earnings.

The way in which women first learn to sew predicates a disjuncture between the work and actual jobs. This learning context also helps to establish a strong link between professional attitudes and traditional female gender roles. The socialization process constructs female gender roles through the acquisition of knowledge aimed at reproducing the family unit. Homeworking women usually learned sewing at a very early age. However, girls do not learn how to sew in order to acquire professional training, prepare for the job market, or equip themselves to earn a wage. Rather they learn sewing to provide a service for themselves and other members of the family, as a talent valued in a good housekeeper. As one fifty-three-year-old woman recalled, "I had a great longing to be a dressmaker, at least to make my clothes. My mother had a small sewing machine, I don't know if you know it, a small machine handpowered. I started to sew at eight years of age, making doll clothes. I broke many needles! But I had this leaning toward sewing, like this girl here has. I used to sew and at twelve years I made my first dress. I made a blouse for my mother. And as the saying goes, in a land of the blind, a one-eyed man is king; I starting sewing for our poor neighbors. I didn't charge anything, you know. I used to make dresses for old ladies, blouses for children...." When, later in life, such women transform their knowledge into an economic resource, they do not necessarily change the perception that they themselves and their families have of the nature of their labor. They continue to view sewing as a housewifely activity and a feminine talent.

Their work, however, is often highly skilled. Sewing skills required for waged labor vary depending on the type of market targeted by the firm.[12] High-quality fashion firms put out very sophisticated models, often using more delicate and expensive materials (e.g., silk and linen). These seamstresses must be very experienced and skilled to be able to assemble a large variety of difficult garments. Garments aimed at a more popular market are, of course, simpler. In fact, piece rates paid to seamstresses may vary by up to 500 percent for the same article, depending on the design and raw material.

All the homeworkers assembled garments from already cut and overlocked cloth; most of them also did some finishing operations such as sewing on buttons or making buttonholes and hems. Great experience is necessary to mount the garment correctly; skill as a machinist is also crucial. Although homeworkers supposedly only perform machining work, they in fact engage in much unpaid labor, making adjustments to and preparing materials: Badly cut pieces have to be trimmed, and sophisticated models need hand stitching before machining. The women recognized their own skill. A forty-year-old woman recalled, "They put the sample in our hand, without explaining anything. Inside the workshop the girls get the models explained by the designer…, not us. We go out with the finished garment in our hand. Full of secrets. You have to find out how to do it, you understand? Then you do it all up and return to the workshop as fast as you can. When you arrive, well, it's an eternity. They start to verify the clothes to see if they're well made, they look, they measure. You start feeling like a 'war of nerves.' In a while you will have to sit at the machine and do some repairs…. They only pay you after the repairs. That money is almost not worth it. But we need it."

Homeworkers did an extremely varied range of work. They rarely brought home the same model two weeks in a row and frequently had to assemble two or three different models in the same week. This constant change of styles added to the difficulty of the assembly operation, for they needed to assemble a few examples of each model before attaining their normal work rhythm.

The employer usually provided all necessary supplies, but in some cases the worker had to obtain the thread. All of the workers owned their sewing machines and many owned two or more. These were regular domestic sewing machines, which are versatile and can make buttonholes, sew zippers, and make different types of stitches. But many homeworkers also had an industrial sewing machine. Possession of an industrial machine usually represented a greater commitment to homeworking because their greater speed allowed a substantial increase in productivity.

Homeworkers associated variations in their earnings with the quantity and quality of the work they did and the piece rates they received. The connections between these factors, however, were not always clear. Homeworkers tried to find the best connections, but close investigation of their actual practice shows that the type and amount of work they received each week and their rate of pay were outside their control.

Homeworkers believed that quantity of work was related to their capacity for work, although in fact the factory determined the amount of work in terms of seasonality of demand and, consequently, of production. Another nearly forgotten factor also influenced quantity of work—the amount a woman could carry to and from the factory. The return trip was especially troublesome because the volume of assembled clothes is larger than that of bundles of cloth taken home and can be quite cumbersome to carry by public transport.

Homeworkers also felt that quality of work determined earnings. This point relates to homeworkers' perceptions of their own skills and their awareness of how they had to find suitable work to maintain their income. Several women were reluctant to accept low-quality work from larger factories because they felt that they could not adapt to a faster rhythm to compensate for lower piece rates. They claimed that they aimed at perfection, not speed, a position consistent with their feelings about sewing as a craft.

The setting of piece rates by the owners, on the other hand, appeared quite baffling to the homeworkers, who could not see any rational basis for increases or decreases. The majority never knew the piece rate before delivering the finished garment; they also were unaware of the price the piece would be sold for. They rarely had access to this information, and when they did, they expressed astonishment, for even when compared with wholesale prices, piece rates were very low indeed. In the few cases where a comparison could be made, rates paid to homeworkers were between 3 and 4 percent of the total wholesale price of the finished garment.

Frequent change of jobs, therefore, was related to attempts to strike an even balance between better-paid, higher-quality, and more constant work. Homeworkers had very little influence or bargaining power in establishing these variables. Their only possibility for improvement was to change jobs.[13] Homeworkers, therefore, show a very stable relation to their work but not to their employers. This apparent contradiction between job dissatifaction and work loyalty is resolved when one realizes that the labor process in homework can be more satisfying than that in a "classic" employment situation. All homeworkers, for example, mounted the whole piece of clothing, avoiding the advanced fragmentation of labor in the large garment factories. They had a good knowledge of the production process as a whole and had relative autonomy in relation to actual tasks performed.

Possessing a skill that is usually seen as a talent, these workers seem to maintain a positive relationship to their work even though they may not be satisfied with their jobs. Pressed by the fact that their family depends on their pay for important items of consumption, they actively search for better opportunities, defined as small increases in piece rates or a more constant flow of work. Despite the lack of a formal contract, the employers maintained close control over important aspects of the work: They determined the quantity, the quality, and the deadline of the work to be done. The lack of efficient mechanisms for negotiation between employers and homeworkers left job turnover as the only way to raise income.

The women thought not about a future career but about the short-term advantages gained from homeworking. In spite of pride in their sewing abilities, they maintained a highly instrumental relationship to their jobs. For them, work represented an essential contribution to family well-being.

The Space and Time of Homework

The space and time of homework is the space and time of the family. Homeworkers showed clearly that family obligations determined their working hours. A forty-five-year-old mother of four children described her daily routine: "I wake up at five in the morning. I sit at the machine and sew until seven. Then I have my breakfast, make breakfast for the children, give the orders to organize the house and all the services, I always do. Around eleven, eleven thirty, I finish making lunch. Only to give the final touches. I finish lunch, give lunch, lunch myself, and sometimes I have time for a ten-minute nap. Then I start working again. And only leave at night for coffee. At that time everybody is at home. More or less at seven everybody is at home. Then I start again at ten, ten thirty."

Another woman, with three sons, further revealed the interpenetration of household duties and paid labor experienced by homeworkers. She explained, "I do like this. In the morning I wake up and take the small one to school, at seven o'clock. When I come back, I tidy the house. When it's nine o'clock, more or less, I sit down at the machine. Eleven I get up and see to the food. Usually I leave it ready from the day before. Now, the older boy tidies the kitchen…. The other one does it at night."

Given the way that paid labor becomes part of everyday life, one cannot understand homework without an analysis of the family and its social relations. These include the central relations of husband and wife, parents and children, but also the many other relatives and individuals who compose the contemporary Brazilian family. As we discuss later, dividing domestic chores—"giving the orders to organize the house and all its services"—is necessary if a woman wants to spend more time in front of her sewing machine. Relations within the family determine what chores she shares and with whom. She must also be able to ask for help in her paid work if things get out of hand. The homeworkers we studied worked on their own but could, when pressed with too much work, ask daughters or daughters-in-law to help them.

Ambiguity of time and space characterize homework. Having a room exclusively for the work is not the norm: Only 42 percent of the interviewees had one. The majority worked in the kitchen or living room, places that need constant tidying. Some did not even have a fixed place for sewing and would install the sewing machine in a different place each day, depending on family routine.

Paid, household, and other family work overlapped so much that all the women had great difficulty establishing how much time they dedicate to their paid work.[14] Although they valued flexibility, this same flexibility seemed to lead to extension of working hours. They expressed similar imprecision in relation to the costs of homeworking: transportation, electricity, and machine maintenance.

Such lack of systematic knowledge stems from the nature of homework itself. Piece rates, flexible hours, and immersion in the domestic sphere all diminish the control of the homeworker over productivity and working conditions. Imprecision also results from weak professional identities and lack of autonomy within the family. That is, the productive labor of homeworking women depends on the normative patterns of domestic work, understood as the amount of time and work dedicated to satisfying the demands of the domestic group and the house. Domestic work appears as a corollary to gender roles. These roles include emotional and affective relations regulated by a normative system that exists beyond purely rational choices. Industrial homework seems subordinated to the organization of family life, with the motivation of workers firmly anchored in their gender roles. As a consequence, homework ends up being performed in accordance with the same principles that regulate domestic work.

The Household Division of Labor

The literature on women and development often argues that the greater a woman's economic power, the greater her decision-making power within the family and the greater the variety of her options.[15] But self-image or identity can shape the meaning of wage labor; professional or wage-earning activity can be undervalued if a woman's identity lacks autonomous development but is instead rooted in traditional expectations and gender hierarchies. Homework exemplifies this process of undervaluation. Its close association with domestic work diminishes its professional legitimacy not only at the macrolevel in the hierarchy of professions but also in the perceptions of other family members. Therefore, there is no guarantee that earning an income will have a positive impact on a woman's relative power within the family. The power a woman can gain from wage earning depends upon the status her occupation has within the normative systems of both family and society, of which the control of economic resources is only one aspect.

Although domestic life is not restricted to "reproductive" activities (such as food preparation, cleaning, and child care), its organization is so strongly based on gender that any change in assigned duties appears as a sign of change in the power relations between men and women. We asked all interviewees to report who was responsible for a variety of basic domestic chores in their home: Was a task their sole responsibility, shared with another person, or solely the responsibility of someone else (and, if so, who was this other person)? Tables 6.1 and 6.2 present the distribution of household chores. Homeworkers undertook most

Table 6.1: The Household Division of Labor: Activities by Person Responsible

Activity	Person Responsible (expressed as % of the time spent on the activity)		
	Homeworker	Homeworker and Others	Others
Child care	78.9	17.6	3.5
Helping children with homework	81.7	16.6	1.7
Washing	63.0	18.0	19.0
Ironing	61.0	21.0	18.0
Shopping	59.0	25.0	16.0
Cooking	68.0	21.0	11.0
Washing dishes	63.0	21.0	16.0
House cleaning	62.0	23.0	15.0
Taking children to the doctor	85.5	12.7	1.8

of the domestic labor in their households. From the perspective of the gender division of labor, homework does not appear to alter significantly the traditional differentiation and specialization of domestic activities. When homeworkers do manage to share or delegate functions, very different patterns emerge in relation to the aid of husbands, mothers, daughters, maids, or relatives. Sons and daughters, but especially daughters, are an important help in cleaning the house or washing up, anticipating their future housekeeping role.

The pattern of male participation in domestic work shows that the men's presence is more striking in activities that entail social interaction, such as child care and education (helping children with homework) or intermediation between family and public worlds such as shopping or taking children to the doctor. Their participation declines sharply the more an activity demands manual, repetitive, or solitary labor such as washing and cleaning. Husbands participate in household activities involving monetary exchanges, where deciding family consumption comes into play.

"Maids" have an important presence in some domestic activities. We must remember that this term in Brazil covers very different situations, such as paying a day worker to do the heavy cleaning or a neighbor to do the washing. Occasionally a family pays a young girl to live in and help with the children. In all cases, maids perform the less interactive and more unskilled functions that require minimal contact with the public world. Thus, husbands are least likely to help with activities that maids can do. Brazilian households perceive the maid as providing a service not to the family as a whole but only to the woman

Table 6.2: Identity of Helpers in Specific Activities

Activity	Helpers					
	(expressed as % of the total amount of time the homeworker is helped)					
	Husband	Children	Maids	Relatives	Mother	Each one does it for themselves
Child care	30.8	23.1	15.4	7.7	23.1	—
Helping children with homework	60.0	20.0	—	—	20.0	—
Washing	5.4	35.1	35.1	10.8	8.1	8.1
Ironing	7.7	33.3	33.3	10.3	7.7	7.7
Shopping	45.2	26.2	4.8	14.3	9.5	-
Cooking	9.4	37.5	9.4	18.8	21.9	3.1
Washing dishes	8.1	54.1	8.1	16.2	10.8	2.7
Housecleaning	7.9	50.0	10.5	15.8	13.2	2.7
Taking children to the doctor	71.4	—	—	28.6	—	—

— = not applicable

of the house. It seems, therefore, that when a woman shares household chores with her husband or maid, this sharing reproduces the differentiation and specialization of wives, husbands, and maids, maintaining the traditional power relationships within the family group. The income-earning activities of the homeworkers do not affect their main obligation for housework, but they can share that labor with a female surrogate, the maid.

Gendered Life Stories and Family Projects

Industrial workers in Latin American countries have much more diversified and unpredictable employment histories than their European or American counterparts. A typical history would include a first period of informal or unstable activities, followed by a relatively long period of work in the formal sector during which time workers save sufficient money to establish themselves in the third phase as independent entrepreneurs, more often than not in the informal sector.[16]

This model, however, is a typically masculine one. Women homeworkers have very different employment life histories. A significant group of such women showed much higher instability in passing through different occupations. They usually started their working lives as live-in maids and then worked in commerce or unskilled industrial jobs before starting to do homework.[17] With the exception of those who had worked in garment factories as machinists, sewing skills were not a professional asset before they began homeworking. Survey questionnaires could not uncover the motivation behind these job changes. However, in-depth interviews and case studies reveal the importance of what could be called "family projects" in these women's choice of homework.

Many women regarded marriage as an important turning point because it usually implied a change in living area, a disruption of an established network of social relations, and the presence of a husband who valued or demanded their staying at home. Some postponed the beginning of homework until a few years after marriage. One woman, twenty-five years old, recounted, "When I came to Rio, I came to work as a maid. When I arrived, I met my husband and married quickly…. I went to my house and never worked again (for seven years)…. He didn't want, he said, 'Look, don't start working because you won't be able to stop.' He doesn't like me working because I pay very much attention to my work and not to him and the kids, and he doesn't like that. He wants, I have to stop. But I earn my money, I am always postponing."

For such women, homework became associated with the dream of having their own houses. The buying or construction of a house strongly motivated many to start earning an income. Another group of women managed to continue working as wage workers outside the home for a longer period after marriage but were forced to turn to homework after the birth of a third or fourth child. Economic consideration motivated their homework; a thirty-year-old woman reported:

> At that time I worked at X (pharmaceutical plant)…. I worked three, almost four years…. When I married, I still worked two or three months…. But then I got pregnant with my first girl and came to live here…. I had to go to work every day, and my husband didn't like it at all. Before we moved, I used to live very near the plant, in half an hour I was there. From here, having to wake up early, with housework and all, I started arriving late, and then I got pregnant…. I then started to sew for friends, for my sister-in-law. I started sewing around here. After some time, when my boy was already born, he [her husband] became unemployed, and it really got bad. We were paying rent…then we went to my mother's house…. But in that time he was unemployed for eight months…. It was then that I started to do homework…. I cannot work in a factory, my husband is very boring, he says that a woman should not work outside the home and all that. At the beginning he didn't like it, now he…. It was a bad fight. He really didn't want it. But one needs it…. I am used to having my things…there's the kids, there is always the need to buy some fruit, clothes, and all.

A second significant group of women showed a very different pattern. Forty-two percent of the homeworkers had never worked outside the home. All their working life had taken place at home, sewing for family or friends or doing homework for the garment industry. For these women, who are totally involved with their domestic role, homework appeared to be the only possibility for earning a real income. A fifty-four-year-old remembered that upon marriage, she "went to live at Bonsucesso [suburb].... With that machine, I used to make dresses for friends, and I made my own dresses and my mother's.... Then I sold that machine and bought a Phillips, but then I got ill. We moved to Penha [a more central neighborhood]. There I had a lot of clients.... Then we came here, we moved to this place and no more clients. There was no one here at that time." Another woman, only twenty-eight, had sewed since her youth, "but to firms, boutiques, as now, only three years.... When I was thirteen I started doing outwork. I had a friend who brought me fifteen, twenty dresses.... It was my mother's machine.... Then I started going steady, at fourteen, and my father bought me a sewing machine."

The possibility of providing children with a higher level of consumption than is possible with their husband's earnings apparently motivated all these women. Small children need better food (vegetables and meat), clothing, and school materials. If there are young adults, the problem of paying for education becomes pressing. Because of the perverse pattern of public education in Brazil, social groups like these, if they want their children to go beyond the eight years of obligatory schooling, usually have to pay for some kind of technical or professional midlevel courses.[18] To be able to provide some kind of additional schooling for their children was therefore an important motivation.

The employment histories of these women differed considerably from those of male industrial workers. First, their passage through wage work was shorter and marked by occupations that lacked promotion or career opportunities. The different phases were not cumulative; experience in a job rarely transferred to the next one. Starting their working lives as live-in maids turned marriage into a positive alternative. The majority of these homeworking women never experienced classical wage work; almost all of their working lives occurred within the domestic realm. For others, an early experience at unskilled factory labor, with harsh discipline and long hours, transformed homework into a pleasant alternative. Such homework cannot be compared to the self-employment of former skilled male factory workers because strong external controls and subordination marked the home employment relation for women.

Homeworkers viewed their own lack of education as an important factor in their persistence at homework.[19] Without the educational assets necessary to look for a better place in the urban market, these women had tried to develop their gender experience into a marketable asset. Some showed a fierce pride in their skills. This professional pride, however, rarely developed into a career orientation. Some had aspirations to become designers or pattern makers or to open their own private workshops. In a highly stratified society like Brazil, cultural and social patterns are very different between social groups, and these homeworkers certainly lacked the sophisticated and internationally highly competitive creative ethos typical of the Brazilian high-middle-class women who were designers and owners of smart boutiques. Their aspirations were therefore distant dreams.

For the greater number of homeworkers, any ambition could interfere in the delicate balance they had managed to establish between their position inside the family and the job market. They did not feel the need for a career. They did not associate pride in work with professional success or recognition by the market or by professional colleagues. To be a good dressmaker was above all a virtue, a sign that a woman was able to realize her female social role.

For many women, homework became the final stage in a life history marked by the absence of a career. For those in middle age, a phase of the life cycle distinguished by important family obligations, homework appeared as a possible compromise between their roles as mothers and wives and the necessity of contributing to the family budget. Older women had other perceptions of homework: Their fragile social situation in the urban market made them regard homework as the only possible way of increasing their meager pensions or retirement pay.

Conclusion: The Domestication of Homework

Among all typically feminine occupations, industrial homework seems to be the most influenced by the gender role of women. Several elements contribute to this. In the first place, the learning process appears natural, with sewing gendered as female. All seamstresses had learned how to sew at a very early age as part of their socialization as future housewives. Only 22 percent had any professional or formal training later on. This naturalization of the training process is one of the important factors for the establishment of a strong link between professional attitudes and traditional female roles. Female roles become constructed through the acquisition of knowledge aimed at the reproduction of the domestic unit. Learning how to sew originally appears as an asset for the future role of wife and mother rather than as an aspect of professional training. Transforming this knowledge into an economic asset does not seem to change the perceptions that homeworkers and their families have of such skill.

Second, the motivation that leads to homework is clearly linked to possible contributions to the family budget. Homeworkers were not the only family breadwinner; in general, they earned less than their husbands. However, they clearly understood the importance of their earning to the family budget. Finally, the same principles that devalue domestic work mark the organization of homework. This means that such labor is not perceived as professional work and is consequently not valued in the purely rational terms of costs and benefits. Ultimately, the domestication of industrial homework weakens the worker's chances of having her labor for the market perceived as a professional activity.

By considering the sexual division of labor and using gender as an explanatory category, we have been able to uncover relations between the sphere of work and other dimensions of social life. Gender socialization and family dynamics seem to mold the productive practices of homeworking women. Homework allows contribution to the family budget without interfering with family and domestic roles. This type of work reinforces the ideology of domesticity. Working alone, with infrequent contact even with employers, without career or promotion prospects, ignored by trade unions and excluded from social benefits usually provided to wage workers, these women find great difficulty in separating their work identity from their roles as mothers and wives.

For these women, industrial homework—although an important contribution to the family budget—does not significantly change the division of labor within the domestic group. They remain responsible for most domestic chores. When they share such chores with others, a clear-cut hierarchy persists between typically male and female activities. Employers also benefit from the logic of domesticity that maintains workers at home and disciplines them into a stable work force. Because they must act within very clearly defined limits, in a context of economic and gender subordination, the women interviewed maintain a delicate balance between the necessity of having paid work and the maintenance of the traditional role of wife and mother inside the domestic group. Industrial homework seems to offer specially favorable conditions for this equilibrium.

Notes

1 Recent data from the ILO showed that homework has a female participation rate of 90 to 95 percent in Germany, Greece, Ireland, Italy, and Holland. In France the rate is 84 percent, in Spain 75 percent, and in England 70 percent. In Brazil, a 1990 household survey showed that 82.2 percent of the 2,826,662 people working in their own homes were women. For a review of recent literature, see Alice Rangel de Paiva Abreu, *O Avesso da Moda: Trabalho a Domicílio na Indústria de*

Confecção (São Paulo: Hucitec, 1986); and Alice Rangel de Paiva Abreu and Bila Sorj, "Trabalho a domicílio nas sociedades contemporâneas: Uma revisão da literatura recente," in *O Trabalho Invisível: Estudos sobre trabalhadores a domicílio no Brasil*, eds. Alice Rangel de Paiva Abreu and Bila Sorj (Rio de Janeiro: Rio Fundo, 1993), pp. 11–24.

2   The literature has stressed economic factors, especially the flexibility gained from a form of work relations that allows employers to solve problems related to changes in consumer markets; reduce production costs through the transfer of space, energy, and equipment costs to the workers themselves; and simultaneously reduce labor costs through informal or illegal labor contracts.

3   This chapter derives from material gathered in two different research efforts. The first was a case study conducted by one of the authors in 1979 (see Abreu, *O Avesso da Moda*); the second was a survey of one hundred home-based seamstresses in Rio de Janeiro carried out as a joint project financed by the Ford Foundation in 1990–1991 (see Abreu and Sorj, eds., *O Trabalho Invisível*). We identified homeworkers through address lists supplied by three garment firms as well as through coworkers during interviews. Percentages mentioned in the text come from this second survey.

4   See Danièle Kergoat, *Les Ouvrières* (Paris: Le Sycomore, 1982), p. 16.

5   The Brazilian garment industry follows international patterns in many aspects. It has a highly heterogeneous structure, with a few large plants for more easily industrialized products using the latest technology and a large number of medium- and small-sized plants that are more labor intensive. It has always been a big employer of women, with more than 80 percent women workers. Dressmaker is still one of the most important female occupations, accounting for more than 7.5 percent of the female labor force in 1990. Small fashion workshops were responsible for the development of women's fashion clothes over the past twenty years. See Abreu, *O Avesso da Moda*, pp. 102–124.

6   The last Brazilian census with direct information about homeworkers was in 1940. At that time, the garment industry incorporated 45 percent of all homeworkers, 82.2 percent of whom were women. See Abreu, *O Avesso da Moda*. Using indirect measurements, Edward Telles showed that in 1980 seamstresses composed the second largest group of women active in the informal sector, representing 7.1 percent of the total. Domestics composed the largest group. See Edward D. Telles, "Características Sociais dos Trabalhadores Informais: O caso das Áreas Metropolitanas no Brasil," *Estudos Afro Asiáticos* 19 (1990): 61–80.

7   There is no systematic survey of labor court processes, so no hard data is available about homeworkers' success in their claims. Personal contacts and interviews with lawyers established, however, that when homeworkers prove their long-term relationship with a firm, they usually get a favorable ruling.

8   In the 1990–91 survey, we found that garment firms hired 93 percent of homeworkers directly, while 78 percent worked on their own. Those who had some kind of help were aided by daughters or mothers.

9   In our 1990–1991 survey, 64 percent were more than 40 years old, 80 percent had a husband or a male partner living with them, and 53 percent had children age fifteen or younger.

10   See Cristina Bruschini, "Crescimento e Crise: Trabalho das brasileiras, paulistas e nordestinas, de 1970 a 1985," *Ciência e Cultura* 42, 3/4 (March/April 1990): 226–247.

11   See Rubem César Fernandes, *Censo Institucional Evangélico—CIN* (Rio de Janeiro: Núcleo de Pesquisas do ISER, 1992), p. 13. We are aware that the high percentage of Evangelicals found among homeworkers could be the result of the design of our survey, based on networks, but it suggests that further investigation is needed to explore the relations between homework and religious patterns in Brazilian society.

12   Based on a rough classification of firms in the 1990–1991 survey, 34 percent of homeworkers worked for the high-quality fashion shops and 52 percent for lower-quality garment firms. It was impossible to determine the type of firm worked for in 14 percent of the cases. The 1979 case study was carried out among five high-quality fashion workshops, and all the women interviewed at that time did quality work.

13   Among the homeworkers interviewed, 72.3 percent had worked for other firms: 37.3 percent in only one other, 23.7 percent in two others, and 38.3 percent in three or more. Of those who had changed jobs, 86.7 percent said they left of their own free will: 33 percent of these because of low wages; 10.3 percent to marry. It seems, however, that the type of work influenced these reasons: 88.5 percent of the women working for high-quality fashion firms, doing very skilled work, said they would not like to work inside the firm.

14   Only 22.2 percent of homeworkers interviewed reported working less than forty hours a week, 44.5 percent between forty and sixty hours, and 33 percent more than that. More than half (56 percent) worked weekends.

15   See Rae Lesser Blumberg, "Towards a Feminist Theory of Development," in *Feminism and Sociological Theory*, ed. Ruth A. Wallace (London: Sage Publications, 1989), pp. 161–199.

16   See Bruno Lautier, "Cycles de vie, trajectoires professionnelles et stratégies familiales: Quelques réflexions méthodologiques à partir de travaux latino-américains," mimeo, 1990; and Robert Cabanes, "Filières et stratégies socio-professionnelles (Étude de cas de douze ouvriers à São Paulo, Brésil)," *Cahiers des Sciences Humaines*, 23, 2 (1987): 163–181.

17   Fifty-seven percent had worked in other types of jobs before doing homework: 25 percent as domestic help, 17.7 percent as unskilled factory workers (12.3 percent in the garment industry), and 17.5 percent at low-level positions in commerce, such as salesgirls.

18   Education in Brazil is obligatory until the age of fourteen (i.e., eight years of schooling). After that, there are few public schools and usually only higher-class students, who tend to perform better academically, get access to these. The same

is true for technical schools, although they reach a different public (urban lower middle classes). This pattern is even more pronounced at the university level. Thirty percent of available places are in good public universities, accessible primarily to the higher classes, and 70 percent in private universities of lower academic prestige.

19 Sérgio da Costa Ribeiro, "Pedagogia da Repetência," *Estudos Avancados* 4, 12 (1991): 18–28, showed that for Brazil as a whole more than half the population had at least six years of education. Only 32 percent of dressmakers interviewed had as many years of schooling. Thirty-four percent of the Brazilian population had eight years of education, while only 17 percent of the seamstresses had done so. Finally, 25% of the Brazilian population finished high school, while only 17% of the seamstresses had done so.

7

"Bibi Khanum"

Carpet Weavers and Gender Ideology in Iran

« *Zohreh Ghavamshahidi*

My grandmother used to get up before the sun rose. I remember when she washed her hands and face with cold water for the morning prayer. Then she woke up everybody. Dad would quickly leave the house to go to the field. He used to drag my two older brothers with him. My two sisters and I were just one year apart, and I was the oldest girl. I don't even remember how old I was when I started weaving, but I know I was not tall enough to sit on the bench in front of the loom. My grandmother taught me how to weave. She told my sisters and I that weaving and sewing are arts. All the girls who want to become a lady (*khanum*) with servants in their husbands' homes should learn to weave and sew. I wondered why she and my mother, who knew how to weave, did not become ladies. We didn't have servants. We all worked around the house, helping in cooking and washing, bringing water from the spring, weeding the vegetables in the garden, and weaving carpets. In our village all the girls knew how to weave. Those who weaved well could find better husbands. I married when I was fourteen. Soon after, my husband and I came to Tehran. He found work at a construction site, and I weaved at home in my spare time. I had to take care of my three children. My youngest was a sick boy, and he died soon after his father's death at the construction site. Weaving became our major source of income. It was not enough; my oldest boy went to work in a restaurant and my daughter helped me weaving. Now they are

both married and gone. I am seventy-eight years old. I weave one small carpet a
year, ordered by this lady from uptown. With the money from the carpet and my
son's assistance, I get by. I still wonder about what my grandmother said about
weaving and becoming a lady.[1]

POOR WOMEN ENGAGE IN HOME-BASED INDUSTRIES BECAUSE OF THEIR SOCIAL
class and gender. Lack of opportunities in education, training, and employment as well as persistent patriarchal ideology lead lower class women to
become unpaid workers or homeworkers with small incomes. Homework is
the strategy employed by their families to solve the contradiction between
gender ideology, that is, men as breadwinners and women as housewives, and
the harsh economic realities that compel women to generate cash income.
Exploitative relationships in the home-based carpet industry in Iran result
from capitalist penetration into the home and a patriarchal gender ideology
that maintains dominant-subordinate social relations in the household.

This study is an empirical microanalysis of the home-based handwoven carpet industry in Iran based on fieldwork conducted at two sites: Najaf-Abad and
Klar. It draws its theoretical framework from the literature on women and
development, especially works focusing on industrial homework and gender
ideology and on Iranian women.[2] I will first focus on the nature of the carpet
industry and the process of the research and then explain the Iranian gender
ideology and the organization of homework.

Carpet Industry and Sexual Division of Labor

The handwoven carpet is a traditional craft in Iran. Historically women in
nomadic tribes carried out carpet weaving. Weaving spread to villages when
nomads, voluntarily or as a result of state policies, settled in remote areas.
Iranian carpets found an expanding domestic and international market in the
late nineteenth century as a result of trade with Europe. Changes then emerged
in the mode of carpet production and the relations of production. Weaving
became a more distinct form of production, which made the home into a workplace for an industry with an international market. European interest in this
industry also changed the organization of production. To assure the quality of
carpets and the range of sizes, the workers came under close supervision. The
large Western market revived the carpet industry in traditional weaving areas.[3]
Carpet weaving became an occupation for women as well as for men at home,
in village workshops, and in factories.

During Pahlavi rule (1921–1979) and the Islamic Republic (since 1979), carpets ranked among Iran's most popular nonoil export items. While Iranian
carpet exports declined after the revolution of 1979, there was a sharp reversal

Table 7.1: Carpet Exports From Iran (in 1,000 Tons and Million Rials)

	1979–1980	1980–1981	1981–1982	1982–1983
Weight	7.9	5.2	2.2	1.0
Value	28,789	30,273	11,894	5,634

	1983–1984	1984–1985	1985–1986	1986–1987
	1.8	2.5	3.7	8.2
	7,184	8,104	10,050	28,217

Source: *Iran Year Book* 1988, p.299

in this trend after 1985; in 1987 handwoven carpets made up 54 percent of total nonoil exports.[4] Table 7.1 indicates the recent trends in carpet exports, demonstrating Iran's increased reliance on handcraft industries.

Under the economic policies of the Islamic Republic, carpet weaving is divided into three different modes: public, private, and cooperative. In all three modes the organization of production includes workshops, factories, and homework. Private investment in carpet weaving at home belongs to the informal economy, which produces a large volume of carpets and escapes unionization and government regulation. Because informal production is an underground activity, there are few official statistics regarding working conditions or wages.

An estimated six million people are directly or indirectly involved with carpet production. Many are dependent on weaving for their livelihoods; for others, such labor generates extra cash for the support of their families.[5] An estimated 90 percent of carpet weavers in villages are women,[6] of whom the majority are between the ages of twelve and forty-five. The women over the age of forty-five who engage in carpet weaving are often widowed.

Carpet production at home has developed two systems: a putting-out system, which operates through vertical contracts and subcontracts, and an independent system, which consists of self-employment. Both systems are forms of an informal economy that mostly uses female labor. Such weaving is tedious and labor intensive and generates a low income. It is a survival activity, linked to home, for landless women in rural areas and the urban poor.

The mode of recruiting women to carpet weaving demonstrates the interrelations between gender ideology and capitalism, with strong emphasis on the sexual division of labor as women do the work at home and men handle the transactions outside the home. Men—the middleman, contractor, and husband or other male relatives—organize all aspects of production and provide the connection between the employer and the worker, even among the self-employed.

Process of Research

During the summer of 1991, I conducted formal interviews with government officials, carpet merchants, and middlemen as well as informal interviews with carpet weavers. I also engaged in participant observation through fieldwork in two sites, Najaf-Abad and Klar.[7] I chose Najaf-Abad and Klar for two reasons. First, I had prior knowledge of the concentration of migrant carpet weavers from Kashan.[8] I also had contacts who assisted me in setting up interviews. A carpet merchant in Tehran who owns a large plot of commercial land in Klar-Abad provided information about Klar and the women carpet weavers. Second, each place represented a specific context for home-based carpet weaving: one rural and one an urban ghetto.[9] In both sites, I met informants through a relative. Some were acquaintances of women I had already interviewed. I interviewed the weavers during the daytime hours when their husbands were out working, using a screening technique; that is, asking them about their daily life, specifically home carpet making. Because many of the women did not acknowledge time spent on weaving as "waged labor"—or, as one put it, "We don't work; weaving is not work; it is something we have to do to help the family"—I had to deduce from their daily activities how much time they spent weaving and treat that time as time spent on a cash-income-generating activity.[10]

Najaf-Abad, in southeast Tehran, is an urban ghetto. Although it has electricity and running water, it is underdeveloped, densely populated, unsanitary, and has a high crime rate. Families live in very small houses or in compounds. Most of the people in this site are migrants from rural areas who have moved to Tehran in search of industrial work since government centralization in the 1940s under the Pahlavi regime. Of twelve women interviewed at this site, three were self-supporting widows working full time at home. Husbands had abandoned two of the women, who then became heads of their households. These women worked part time at home and part time outside the home as domestic help and public baths workers. The other women, who had joint incomes with their husbands, worked both outside and inside the home.[11] Some worked as tailors and some as laundresses.

The second site, Klar, is a village near the small but rapidly developing town of Klar-Abad in a northern province. Despite the rapid urbanization of Klar-Abad as a result of a summer housing development, the characteristics of a rural area continue to exist in nearby villages. Of the twenty-five women interviewed at this site, two were self-supporting widows working outside and inside the home, and six had been abandoned by male partners and worked both outside and inside their homes. Seventeen women had joint incomes with their husbands and worked both at home and outside. Most of these women worked as domestic servants in Klar-Abad.

Table 7.2: Characteristics of Women Carpet Weavers in Najaf-Abad and Klar

Site	Number of Families	Family Size	Age of Weavers	Literacy among Weavers (%)
Najaf-Abad	12	1–7	16–75	80
Klar	25	4–8	12–45	40

The weavers fell into three different groups: widows who were heads of the household; women who had been abandoned and were heads of the household; and families with joint incomes. Of the thirty-seven women interviewed at the two sites, thirteen were female heads of household, and they suffered most from lack of finances. Table 7.2 breaks down each site according to the number of families, family size, age, and level of literacy. Family size includes the members of the nuclear family as well as, in some cases, in-laws. The table demonstrates that the average family size of weavers in the rural area is larger than that in the urban area. This discrepancy may be the result of women's access to birth control and family planning in urban areas. The larger families in the rural areas tend to have more than one weaver, which may explain the younger ages of weavers in rural areas as compared to those in the urban areas. The female children in the urban area attend primary and secondary schools; those in the rural area only have access to primary school. The literacy rate in the rural area is, as expected, half that of the urban area. This difference may be the result not only of Iranian gender ideology but also of uneven development in the countryside.

Iranian Gender Ideology and the Feminization of Homework
In order to understand women's subordinate position in home-based carpet production, it is necessary to study Iranian gender ideology and its interrelations with capitalism. The socialist feminist literature on patriarchy contributes to the understanding of the relationship between patriarchy and class under capitalism.[12] However, because carpet weaving has been a production process under nomadic and agrarian as well as capitalist systems in Iran, there is a need for a broader definition of patriarchy that takes into account a specific historical reality and the experiences of the masses within a specific culture. As Lourdes Benería and Martha Roldán explained, gender ideology includes the ranking of traits and activities in a way that grants males superior value and thus more access to resources that generate continued male domination and female subordination.[13] Patriarchy can be defined as a set of beliefs and attitudes that generate male power, a historical and cultural-religious system that is socially constructed. It is neither static nor monolithic; it changes and varies

across culture and the stages of socioeconomic development. It is based in part on the sexual division of labor.

According to Deniz Kandiyoti, classical patriarchy of the extended agrarian society grants the senior male the utmost authority over everyone else. The most important unit of a classic patriarchy is the patrilocal extended family.[14] Reproduction of the labor force is central for the maintenance of the classical patriarchy and its socioeconomic system. Women's subordination in this system is linked to women's role as a medium for forming family alliances through marriage. Islam emphasizes family as the most important building block of social structure and motherhood as the most important responsibility for women. This emphasis creates a sexual division of labor based on gender hierarchy: women as caregivers at home and men as breadwinners and protectors of family honor. This arrangement limits women's growth in the socioeconomic, political, and cultural spheres. The high value attached to women's fecundity and filiation ties are characteristic both of classic patriarchy and of Islamic gender ideology.

With the advent of capitalism and the establishment of the nation-state, Iranian gender ideology has gone through a historical transformation. Although the old form of patriarchy still exists in some areas of Iran, new forms of patriarchy have been (re)constructed as the result of "modernization" and political and socioeconomic changes. New forms of patriarchy continue to grant authority over women to men. These male-female relationships pertain to socioeconomic spheres within as well as outside the household. As Valentine Moghadam noted, "Patriarchal forms of control over women include the institutionalization of extremely restrictive codes of behavior for women, a practice of rigid gender segregation, specific forms of family and kinship, and a powerful ideology linking family honor to female virtue."[15] The state's ideology, whether secular under the Pahlavi regime or theocratic under the Islamic Republic, allocates women a specific role in family, economic, and other public policies. The process of state building during both Pahlavi rule and the Islamic Republic incorporated sexual politics at its center.[16] The state legitimizes and re-creates the image of a perfect woman through all social and political channels.[17]

Formal Islamic and secular laws as well as Iranian customs reinforce classical and modern patriarchy. Secular laws under the Pahlavi regime and Islamic laws under the Islamic Republic have given more privileges to men than to women. Although the Family Protection Law and Women's Suffrage Act passed under the shah and the number of educated and professional women increased, the position of women in the lower classes did not change. The shah's gender policies were meant to co-opt middle-class women into the system and create a power base for his regime. His ideology of "modernity" imposed images of Western women as role models upon Iranian women. Despite the shift in regime and the establishment of the Islamic Republic, there is continuity in the general gender system that imposes patriarchal control over women and provides men with greater socioeconomic privileges. Although Islamic law grants the right to ownership of property to women, usually it is the husband who makes decisions regarding family income. Under the Islamic Republic, as under the Pahlavi regime, women's public activities have to fit the ideology of the governement.

Under the dominant gender system, the rural classes and the traditional merchant class customarily attach high value to infant boys. Male children receive more attention than female children in their nutrition, education, and emotional support. Low-income classes, especially in rural areas, neglect female children and women's health. In Klar, poor living conditions affected women more harshly than men. Women did not eat until everybody else had eaten and, as a result, often ate much less. The old Iranian saying, "Daughters do not belong to us, they belong to strangers," means that a girl needs the financial, physical, and emotional protection of her father and brothers only until she is given away to marry a stranger. In fact, *stranger* is a proper term because a large percentage of marriages in rural areas and some urban areas are arranged, especially among the low and lower middle classes, and girls do not have much say in the matter. A young married woman is obliged by custom and by Islamic law to obey her husband, devote herself to her children and husband, and, in some cases, take care of elderly in-laws.

Sex-role socialization of children is important for the reconstruction of patriarchy because it prescribes sexual segregation and sexual division of labor and designates the home as women's workplace and the world outside the home as men's workplace. Women and men internalize "proper" male and female behavior, attitudes toward life in general, and their own roles through a complex process of socialization that begins at home.[18] Most decisions pertaining to social interactions are the domain of the male members of the family. "I must ask my husband if I can speak to you or not, because he does not want me to speak to strangers," was the reply I received from a young mother during my fieldwork. My requests for interviews were turned down by several women who did not believe it was proper to speak with me without their husbands' permission.

As part of their sex-role socialization, women and little girls in rural Iran learn homework as an asset for their futures. All weavers at both sites learned the skill at a very young age at home from their mothers or other female relatives. As an older widow carpet weaver in Najaf-Abad explained, "Learning to weave is part of the village women's life. It is considered more an art which occupies the leisure time of the women at home." Embodied in this statement is the myth that encourages girls to learn weaving by enticing them to think of it as art and leisure instead of an essential survival skill. The majority of women interviewed did not regard weaving as formal employment. The weavers described the beauty of their product, recognizing the aesthetic value of the carpets as a craft that satisfied the desire to create something more permanent than the results of mundane daily activities. Many women harbored unfulfilled desires to realize their creative potential and achieve a measure of independence.

Women in both sites, however, wove not because of an intrinsic interest in the art, although they may have wished to do so, but for economic survival. A weaver in Najaf-Abad admitted, "If I do not weave, I will die from hunger, or I will be a beggar on the streets." One of the abandoned women in Klar said, "I have to weave because the money from my work [outside the home] is not enough for the survival of the family." The income generated from carpet weaving at home went directly to household expenses, and the women were left with little or no money for themselves. A young weaver expressed her wishes to weave for herself, saying, "I wish I could weave a beautiful Kashan design carpet for my dowry and take it with me to my future husband's home." Another energetic young weaver wished she could "weave a carpet for myself and sell it and open a beauty shop."

Weaving skill significantly affects the future of young girls, especially their marriage prospects. Since carpet weaving generates income for the family, a young woman without this skill has difficulty finding a suitable husband, especially in the rural areas that historically produce Iranian carpets. "Carpet weavers earn a higher wage by local standards, so a woman skilled in carpet weaving has no problem finding a husband. Less talented women work at lesser crafts, spinning wool into yarn, cleaning hair from the down of Cashmere coats."[19] Yet weaving's importance remains unrecognized, illuminating the larger devaluation of women's work.

When lower-class and lower-middle-class families face economic realities, they are confronted with the contradiction between having women work for income and the ascribed sex roles that discourage women from taking on the role of breadwinner or contributor. One way to solve this contradiction is by having women work at home. Homework is not limited to carpet weaving; women also knit dresses, pullovers, and hats and process pickles and jams. Under this condition capitalism penetrates into the home and takes advantage of patriarchal arrangements that allow the exploitation and oppression of women. The putting-out system is a prime example of capitalist and patriarchal control of women's labor. Iranian gender ideology, that of female subordination and the asymmetrical division of labor at home, is compatible with capitalism, which undervalues women's work by calling it "housework." Women carpet weavers are therefore vulnerable to severe exploitation by an underground economy, which in turn helps to maintain this gender ideology.

The Putting-out System

The putting-out system produces carpets mostly for the national market and, to a lesser degree, for the international market. The carpets are of low and medium quality. The prices vary according to the design, the quality of raw material, the knot density, and the size of the carpet. In the putting-out system, the merchants, who are located in the major trading centers, have no direct contact with the weavers at home.

Merchants contract workers through the mediation of a middleman known to the weavers as the *miyanji*. There are two types of subcontracts. Under horizontal subcontracts, the merchant and the weavers agree to the production plan without the merchant providing raw material. Under vertical subcontracts, the merchant provides the raw material to the weavers at home.[20] The putting-out system depends on vertical subcontracting. In almost all cases, the merchants provide specific instructions.

In traditional urban carpet-weaving centers such as Kashan, Tabriz, and Meshad, the design of the carpets and the quality of the wool and dyes are extremely important. Mr. Mohammed, a miyanji, recounts that "in these regions most often the weavers are supervised by master weavers, known as an *ustad*, hired by the merchant to oversee the production." Most of the carpets woven by women in Najaf-Abad are of the Kashan design, which is rated high in quality in both domestic and international markets. This design needs a high knot density, which requires great skill, much practice, and immense concentration. High-knot-density carpets are usually produced for export. The weavers from this site who had migrated from Kashan said that "up to 70 percent of weavers in Kashan and the villages around this area are under contract with local merchants through a middleman." Furthermore, they stated that "the miyanji comes every week to inspect the design and give further supervision." One woman explained that "the low-knot-density carpets are for the local markets." Each carpet takes twelve to eighteen months to be completed. Another weaver described the process further: "When the carpet is woven, the local merchant or the miyanji transfers it for cleaning and finishing to their workshops and then transfers the carpets to the trading centers which they subcontracted to or return them to the merchant to be sold in the local market." These women had a thorough knowledge of the social and economic organization of their labor.

The miyanji guarantees the wages of weavers through an oral contract. Women earn their wages by piece rate through several payments. Usually the first one is an advance payment of 10 to 12 percent of the total contract. The miyanji pays the rest of the wage at different stages of progress, with the last installment paid upon the completion of the carpet, although some weavers ask for partial payment in advance to support their families. In most cases such advances result in weavers owing labor time to the merchants by the time the carpet is finished. The time owed to the merchant is carried over to the next contract, throwing the weaver into a form of indentured servitude. The weavers explain the reason for these labor time debts: "We make very little money, and whenever they give our wages [installments] we buy food and clothing and some medicine, but everything is getting so expensive that we cannot even save a rial for bad times."

Wages hardly match profits in this system. According to the miyanji, "In some contracts the unit of payment is based on the number of knots tied per row, which varies from region to region. Knots are divided in each row depending on the size of the carpet." In Klar, the putting-out workers tie eight to ten thousand knots a day, for which they receive a wage set by the contractors that varies with the design of the carpet. An average of 220 days a year is spent on each large carpet. It is difficult to determine the weavers' wages according to the knots and rows. If we assume that the workers receive the minimum wage of 760 rials a day, and if at least two workers are engaged in weaving the same carpet, then the annual combined income of both workers is approximately 334,400 rials. After a carpet is finished, it is marketed for between 3.5 to 4.5 million rials.[21]

Subtracting the wages and the raw materials from the price of the carpet leaves the merchant with a great profit that sometimes amounts to ten times the cost of labor and raw materials combined. An overall evaluation of the wages indicates that the wages are very much below the profit realized by the merchant, demonstrating the exploitative nature of employment relations in carpet weaving. The cheap and abundant labor of women born in poverty allows merchants to maintain low costs and high profits.

The low level of family income, rising inflation in the cost of subsistence goods, and rising unemployment leave the weaver with no alternative to home production of carpets under these exploitative conditions. When asked to describe the "bad times," weavers responded in ways that revealed a fatalistic attitude. One confessed, "The miyanji told me I should be very happy that I have a job; anytime now the government may come in and stop the operation and then I will starve to death." Another weaver exclaimed, "God bless Mohammed [the miyanji]; he always chooses me to weave. I think he likes me.

He told me he could choose someone younger and better to replace me, but he doesn't because he trusts me." The carpet-weaving industry seems to operate on a tight network of manipulation and intimidation of the workers. Threatening the weavers with withdrawal of work allows the contractors and the subcontractors to hire workers on their own terms. Playing one weaver against another creates a tense competitive atmosphere, which results in low labor costs. Some weavers are not as passive as others when they are threatened with the loss of their small income. Oftentimes they question and argue with the contractors and subcontractors about the value of their labor. However, "they are mainly ignored or told to take it or leave it," as I was told by a weaver in Klar. A merchant claimed that "these women are sometimes obnoxious about their income…. If I want to pay more money, I hire men who are more dedicated to weaving." He further implied that women have other things to do.

The weavers do not have much moral support outside their own profession. A weaver revealed: "I have no one to talk to. When I tell my husband that I think I should earn more money for my labor, or I tell him I am tired and I am sick, he tells me I am a woman and can't ask for much and I should stop nagging and be thankful that I have a husband and a family. So there is not much I can do, although sometimes I feel like either killing myself or him."

Independent Carpet Weavers

I refer to this system of production as "independent" because the weavers are under neither contract nor subcontract. They produce carpets through their own investments and family labor. I find it difficult to categorize this system as entrepreneurial because the low level of income makes the accumulation of capital virtually impossible. Under the independent system, most of the weavers own tools, looms, and material. Dariush Khan, a carpet dealer or *dallal*, explained that "the independent weavers produce lower-quality and smaller-sized carpets. Because the carpets have a low knot density and are made of low-quality wool and artificial dye, they are sold in the local market to lower-income customers. The carpets have a considerably lower market value than those produced through the putting-out system."

The cheaper carpets are sold faster; as a result, weavers do not experience the risk of getting stuck with the product. The independent production of carpets takes place at home. In addition to fulfilling other household chores, the wife and other female members of the household spend a portion of their time weaving. Most of the weavers also engaged in part-time work outside their homes. In the villages, female heads of the household did small-scale farming and vegetable growing. In Klar, some of the weavers worked in services such as housecleaning and laundry at the upper-class summer homes. In Najaf-Abad, the independent weavers in both groups, the abandoned as well as those married with joint income, worked outside the home. One of the weavers from the joint-income group explained, "I work at a public bath as a *dall'ak* three days a week."[22] Another weaver in the same site, a widow, hesitantly admitted, "Whenever I am short of money I become *sigheh* to a man [temporary marriages, or *mut'ah*]. You see, I know this old lady who knows a lot of lonely men, and she arranges the meeting."[23]

In the villages, the elderly and female children prepare the primary steps for weaving: collecting wool, spinning yarn, and cleaning. Male members of the household assist in dyeing the yarn, adjusting the looms, and setting up the warp. In Najaf-Abad, the independent weavers bought ready-made yarn. In Klar, some male members of the family were also carpet weavers.

There is a great deal of cooperation among the family members, neighbors, and kin in the independent weaving system. The husband, brother, male kin, or miyanji takes the finished product to be sold either to a dealer or at a local market. The husband receives the money for the product in full. He pays the miyanji a commission and takes out costs to reinvest for the next carpet, and the rest of the money is spent for the household. Women without men cannot market their carpets directly. In Najaf-Abad, however, two independent weavers had agreements with a middleman because they had no male family members.

Comparative Study of the Two Systems

In Najaf-Abad, twice as many women engaged in the independent system of production as in the putting-out system. Involved in outside paid work, they chose not to make commitments to subcontractors. In contrast, the number of women in the putting-out system in Klar was almost double the number of independent weavers. This difference may indicate that women in rural areas have less time and access to work outside the home. The widows in both sites relied primarily on home-based work income. One of them received some assistance from the government because her son, who was the head of the household, was killed in the Iran-Iraq War. A son financially assisted another older widow. Abandoned women at both sites seemed to be the most burdened of the three categories because they were heads of households.

Weavers who work under the putting-out system have less control over the process of production than do the independent weavers. In this system, women are confined to their homes and have very little mobility around the house. They usually are isolated from other women and from mainstream social activities and have very little contact with people outside their families. Usually all female members over twelve years of age engage in weaving. Elders, such as the mothers, sisters, or other relatives, supervise the less-skilled females. In the independent system, women are not as secluded and confined to their homes; they exercise more control over the process of production because the weavers have more mobility around or outside the house than do those in the putting-out system and an outsider does not supervise the weavers. They choose the design and the size of the carpet and have more flexibility in choosing the time for weaving. Under both systems, the money from the sale of the carpet goes back to the household, and the women do not enjoy economic independence. Asked about her earnings and how she spends the money, one weaver answered, "I do not even see the money. My husband takes it and pays back our loan and spends it on other things." Another woman from the joint-income group explained, "I take some money from my husband and save it for myself." The independent weaving system appears less exploitative regarding employment relations. However, in terms of how it affects the asymmetrical gender division of labor, it is similar to the putting-out system. Women are still in a subordinate position. In neither system do women market their product; men monopolize the market.

Conditions of Work

Working conditions at home in the rural areas are harsher than in the urban areas.[24] Most rural houses have no electricity, and weavers' houses are damp, dark, and cramped. The average working life cycle of a highly skilled weaver is estimated at thirteen years because the weavers lose their eyesight, in part due to improper lighting. Some weavers who start very young suffer from different types of physical ailments exacerbated by the nature of their work. Weaving is the only skill some women know.[25]

Working conditions create various health hazards. The vertical loom, recognized as safer than the horizontal, still produces health problems. Long hours of sitting on the short benches in front of old and deteriorated looms has cost some weavers their lives. Due to the weight of carpets, looms sometimes collapse on the weavers, causing death or permanent injury. Young weavers often develop abnormalities of the spinal cord, deformed arms and legs, and bone disease. Many pregnant women have stillbirths. Horizontal looms, used among the nomadic tribes and in some villages, also pose a number of hazards. The weavers have to squat in front of these looms on damp floors for hours, which can result in severe deformity in back and hip bones. Weavers working on horizontal looms often have several miscarriages, severe pain, and heavy menstrual bleeding. Combined with the lack of fresh air, particles from the wool can result in various lung diseases. If the weavers use unsanitary wool and chemical dyes, they can contract skin allergies and disease. Infants and young children do not get much care and are neglected due to the heavy workload at home. Bibi Khanum, the weaver in Najaf-Abad quoted at the start of this essay, remembered that "many babies died back then [referring to the 1950s] because their mothers did not have time to feed them or clean them." This problem still exists in most of the remote areas.

Conclusion

This case study of homeworkers demonstrates that women engage in carpet weaving at home because of their gender and social class. Women from lower-income classes in the villages or urban slums do not have access to resources such as education and training for alternative employment and are thus exploited in this industry. They are marginalized and pauperized through the process of capitalist development and are subordinated by a gender ideology that grants privileges only to men. Using gender ideology as a justification for women working at home, the local and national investors, merchants, dealers, and miyanji extract large profits from women's labor. Low-intensity capital investment in carpet weaving at home and low wages due to the informal nature of the industry, along with high prices for the commodity in national and international markets, contribute to the concentration of capital among the miyanji and the merchants. Although the development of the carpet industry promotes employment among women, it neither changes the asymmetrical division of labor at home nor increases their income to the point of improving their social class. The low wages do not allow accumulation of household income but merely contribute to family survival.

This study also reveals that homework reinforces a gender ideology that proclaims that women should be at home, taking care of their children and their homes as their primary responsibility. Men's role as breadwinners and as the protectors of the family creates a belief in men's superiority among family members who downplay the significance of the economic contributions of women. Homework as a solution to economic problems in families does not violate gender ideology and serves to maintain the historical, social, and economic relations in households structured by patriarchy. The asymmetrical sexual division of labor found in this industry demonstrates that women's socioeconomic subordination is maintained through a patriarchal ideology that promotes seclusion and confinement of women at home and defines their role as mothers and wives busy with "housework."

Neither the public nor private sectors of the carpet industry have provided statistics on women weavers, nor have they seriously formulated policies to improve women's economic conditions in this sector. The Islamic Republic has focused on the quality and the export of carpets rather than on the producers of this commodity. Contrary to the euphoric expectations of the Iranian government, gender socioeconomic relations have not changed fundamentally in lower-income families, especially in rural sectors and in urban slums. Women's exploitation and oppression in home-based carpet production most likely will continue as long as the state nurtures and encourages the historical gender ideology in Iran.

Weavers at both research sites believed that their condition could improve if their work was recognized as labor and if there was an increase in education, training, and employment opportunities as well as loan credit. The Islamic Republic must work toward eradication both of exploitative relations of production in the informal economy and of gender ideology. It is necessary to treat carpet weaving as part of the formal economy in order to be able to regulate it. The government should research the weavers' condition and establish women's weaving organizations that would oversee the interests of weavers and report on their working conditions and their needs. The state, employers, and families must emphasize the market value of women's work and fair remuneration for it. Weaving needs to be recognized as skilled work and should be paid an appropriate wage; social benefits should be provided; and weavers should have greater control over their labor, the process of production, and the product. To help change the prevailing gender ideology, it is fundamental to recognize weaving as work and to include its contribution in national economic statistics, educating the public about the role of women in economic production and demystifying the image generally held by the masses about women as housewives and mothers.

Notes

1 I would like to thank Eileen Boris and Lisa Prügl for their editing of this article. My findings have appeared in a different form in *Women's Studies International Forum* under the title "The Linkage of Iranian Patriarchy and the Informal Economy in Maintaining Women's Subordinate Role in Home-based Carpet Production." Bibi Khanum was interviewed in her home in Najaf-Abad in Tehran. She owned her two-story home, which had two rooms on each floor. She lived downstairs and rented the upstairs to a family of four, who had migrated from Kashan, where Bibi Khanum was also from.

2 Ester Boserup's pioneering work clarified that development has a negative effect on the economic status of women and has created not only a gap in productivity between men and women but also a clear-cut division of labor by sex in all societies. See *Women's Role in Economic Development* (New York: Saint Martin's Press, 1970). The literature on women and development is vast: See, for example, Elsa Chaney and Marianne Schmink, "Women and Modernization: Access to

Tools," in *Sex and Class in Latin America*, eds. June Nash and Helen I. Safa (South Hadley, Mass.: Bergin and Garvey Publishers, 1980); Lourdes Benería and Gita Sen, "Accumulation, Reproduction, and Women's Role in Economic Development: Boserup Revisited," *Signs: A Journal of Women in Culture and Society* 7 (Winter 1981): 279–298; Mayra Buvinic, Margaret Lycette, and William McGreevey, eds., *Women and Poverty in the Third World* (Baltimore, Md.: The Johns Hopkins University Press, 1983); Noeleen Heyzer, *Missing Women: Development Planning in Asia and the Pacific* (Kuala Lumpur: Asian and Pacific Development Center, 1985); and Maria Mies, "The Dynamics of Sexual Division of Labor and Integration of Women into the World Market," in *Women and Development: The Sexual Division of Labor in Rural Societies*, ed. Lourdes Benería (New York: Praeger, 1982), pp. 1–28. For scholarship on Iranian women since the 1979 revolution, see Farah Azari, ed., *Women of Iran: The Conflict with Fundamentalist Islam* (London: Ithaca Press, 1983); Gity Nashat, ed., *Women and Revolution in Iran* (Boulder, Colo.: Westview Press, 1983); Nahid Yeganeh and Nikki Keddie, "Sexuality and Shi'i Social Protest in Iran," in *Shi'ism and Social Protest*, eds. Juan R. Cole and Nikki Keddie (New Haven: Yale University Press, 1986), pp. 108–136; Adel K. Ferdows and Amir H. Ferdows, "Women in Shi'i Fiqh: Images Through the Hadith," in *Women and Revolution in Iran*, pp. 55–68; Afsaneh Najmabadi, "Hazards of Modernity and Morality: Women, State, and Ideology in Contemporary Iran," in *Women, Islam and the State*, ed. Deniz Kandiyoti (Philadelphia: Temple University Press, 1991), pp. 48–76; Eliz Sanasarian, *The Women's Rights Movement in Iran* (New York: Praeger, 1982); Janet Afary, "On the Origins of Feminism in Early 20th-Century Iran," *Journal of Women's History* 1 (Summer 1989): 65–87; Lois Beck, "Women Among Qashqa'i Nomadic Pastoralists in Iran," in *Women in the Muslim World*, eds. Lois Beck and Nikki Keddie (Cambridge, Mass.: Harvard University Press 1978), pp. 351–373; Gholam-Reza Vatandoust, "The Status of Iranian Women During the Pahlavi Regime," in *Women and the Family in Iran*, ed. Asghar Fathi (Leiden, Netherlands: E. J. Brill, 1985), pp. 107–113; Janet Bauer, "Demographic Change, Women and the Family in a Migrant Neighborhood of Tehran," in *Women and the Family in Iran*, pp. 158–186; Erika Friedl, *Women of Deh Koh: Lives in an Iranian Village* (New York: Penguin, 1989), pp. 158–186; Valentine Moghadam, "Women, Work, and Ideology in the Islamic Republic," *International Journal of Middle East Studies* 20 (1988): 221–243; and Moghadam, *Modernizing Women: Gender and Social Change in the Middle East* (Boulder, Colo.: Lynne Rienner Publishers, 1993).

3 A. Jerrehian, *Oriental Rugs Primer* (Philadelphia: Running Press, 1980), pp. 22, 192.

4 *Iran's Chamber of Commerce Report* 10 (1986): 34–37; 11 (1987): 28.

5 *Farsh* (publication of the Iranian Corporate Carpet Company [CCCI]) 6 (1986): 2.

6 *Farsh* 13 (1991): 2.

7 Najaf-Abad and Klar are fictitious names. I established contact with weavers through male merchants and middlemen who were introduced to me by my male

relatives. The weavers were in touch with the middlemen and merchants through their husbands or male relatives.

8   Kashan is a town known for its quality handwoven carpets.

9   Most weavers in both sites knew each other. In Najaf-Abad, I started my interview with the widow weaver, Bibi Khanum, who introduced me to other weavers in the neighborhood. In Klar, most weavers were close or distant relatives who were in daily contact with each other, which made the process of research easier. The interviews were very informal, and direct quotations in this paper are taken from both taped conversations and my own recollections. Although some women were extremely cooperative in the interviews, others were suspicious of my motivations and did not agree to taped interviews. Four women weavers in Najaf-Abad did not agree to be interviewed and denied that they were weaving at home despite others' claims that they did.

10 For a model study of patterns of time allocation in households, see Elizabeth King and Robert E. Evenson, "Time Allocation and Home Production in Philippine Rural Households," in *Women and Poverty in the Third World*, pp. 35–62.

11 For demographic information on immigrant areas of south Tehran, see Bauer, "Demographic Change, Women and the Family."

12 Michele A. Barrett, *Women's Oppression Today: Problems in Marxist Feminist Analysis* (London: Verso, 1980); Veronica Beechey, "On Patriarchy," *Feminist Review* 3 (1979): 66–82; and Zillah R. Eisenstein, "Developing a Theory of Capitalist Patriarchy," in *Capitalist Patriarchy and Case for Socialist Feminism*, ed. Zillah R. Eisenstein (New York: Monthly Review Press, 1979), pp. 5–40.

13 Lourdes Benería and Martha Roldán, *The Crossroads of Class and Gender: Industrial Homework, Subcontracting, and Household Dynamics in Mexico City* (Chicago: The University of Chicago Press, 1987), p. 12.

14 Deniz Kandiyoti, "Bargaining with Patriarchy," *Gender and Society* 2 (1988): 274–287.

15 Valentine Moghadam, "Patriarchy and the Politics of Gender in Modernizing Societies: Iran, Pakistan and Afghanistan," *International Sociology* 7 (1992): 37.

16 Afsaneh Najmabadi, in "Hazards of Modernity and Morality," explains how both the Pahlavi shahs and the Islamic Republic created images of modern and modest women.

17 In the 1970s a number of intellectuals, including Ali Shari'ati, have suggested that Fatima, the daughter of the prophet Mohammed, is the role model of a perfect Muslim woman who patiently devoted her life to Islam and her father, husband, and sons. The Islamic Republic holds this model as a valid point of reference in the socialization of children. See Marcoi K. Hermansen, "Fatemeh as a Role Model in the Works of Ali Shari'ati," in *Women and Revolution in Iran*, pp. 87–96.

18 For detailed information on women's life cycle and the process of socialization, see Behnaz Pakizegi, "Legal and Social Position of Iranian Women," in *Women in the Muslim World*, pp. 216–226.

19 Paul English, *City and Village in Iran: Settlement and Economy in Kirman Basin*

(Madison: University of Wisconsin Press, 1966), p. 82.

20 For information on vertical and horizontal industrial subcontracting, see Benería and Roldán, *The Crossroads of Class and Gender*, pp. 31–32.

21 One U.S. dollar equaled 1,600 rials according to the exchange rate at the Central Bank of Iran in 1991.

22 A dall'ak works at the public bathhouses washing the customers' hair and bodies for an unstandardized wage of which she pays a portion to the owner of the bathhouse. It is a rather demeaning profession but widely practiced by rural women migrants in major cities. It should be noted that the public bathhouses in Iran are sexually segregated.

23 Sigheh, or temporary marriage, is practiced among Shi'i Muslims. Most often women are engaged in this marriage for income. For a comprehensive analysis, see Shahla Haeri, *Law of Desire: Temporary Marriages in Shi'i Iran* (Syracuse, N.Y.: Syracuse University Press, 1989).

24 The information regarding work conditions and the related problems is based on isolated lines from different volumes of *Farsh*, also from informal interviews with two carpet experts employed by CCCI, middlemen, and the weavers.

25 *Farsh* 9 (1987): 11.

8

Home-Based Work
as a Rural Survival Strategy
A Central Javanese Perspective

« *Dewi Haryani Susilastuti*

WHEN THE DUTCH COLONIAL ADMINISTRATION CARRIED OUT A CENSUS IN THE nineteenth century, it found that women in many rural areas of Java and Madura performed home-based work as a secondary occupation.[1] During the Dutch occupation as well as after independence, women in Central Javanese villages wove bamboo and made batik and pottery in their homes.[2] Today, home-based industry absorbs a significant portion of the labor force in rural Java.[3] Such industry is particularly important because of the abundant supply of labor in the area.[4]

Informal sector employment, including home-based work, is generally concentrated in urban areas because of the limited ability of the urban formal sector to absorb migrants.[5] However, not every poor person can afford to migrate. More and more landless households in the "Third World" rely on nonagricultural employment in a growing rural informal sector.[6] In Indonesia, rural cottage industries employ most industrial workers and a substantial proportion of underemployed farm workers.[7] Cottage industries have traditionally contracted out work, and home-based work is a prominent feature of the Indonesian countryside.

This study focuses on home-based employment in the garment industry in a village in rural Java. It explores the various types of activities household members engage in to increase household income. Furthermore, it probes the extent to which household size and worker skill determine income.

I chose the garment industry because it has a long history in the area and has served as a widely available source of income. Seasonal fluctuations characterize this industry. Because people dependent on agriculture for their income are the main buyers of clothing produced in the area, demand is highest during the peak agricultural season, usually December and January, and lowest when there is little agricultural employment. Thus, the seasons in garment production coincide with seasons in rice and tobacco growing. Employment opportunities in all sectors are highest during the peak and regular seasons, and the lean season in the garment industry coincides with the "waiting season" in agriculture. During the peak season, those with skills other than sewing prefer to work in nonagricultural jobs outside the garment industry, such as construction, because such work promises a higher income. During the lean season, workers tend to fall back on the garment industry because alternatives are harder to find.

To account for seasonal variations, I collected data during the regular, peak, and lean seasons. Using a structured questionnaire, I interviewed one home-based worker in each household. Because of the high labor turnover, the number of respondents interviewed in each season differed slightly, varying from 272 in the lean season to 298 in the regular season and 301 in the peak season. I also conducted in-depth interviews with twenty workers who had been laboring in the garment industry for more than fifteen years and with local leaders. I obtained additional data through observation and casual conversations with people at the research site.

The Nature of Home-Based Employment

Many home-based workers said that the garment industry has experienced a substantial decline. They complained that over the past five years, the lean season appeared to have become longer and the peak season shorter. Before the garment industry started to decline, local entrepreneurs had invested capital, employing both in-workers and out-workers. Fluctuations in market demand and severe competition from larger firms led these entrepreneurs to rely exclusively on home-based workers. As some entrepreneurs put it, employing in-workers "caused too many hassles." Mr. T., a fifty-five-year-old entrepreneur, remembered: "When we still employed in-workers we had to provide a midday meal for them. We had to limit their working time from eight in the morning to four in the afternoon. We could not ask them to stay later and do more work without giving them extra money. You see, they received

workers do not form opposing poles of "creative" and "routine" work but rather form a continuum (see Table 9.1).[20] Nor are the different kinds of work strictly segregated by sex. Homeworking is more often done for voluntary than involuntary reasons: Given the choice, the majority said they would continue working at home. Thus, for most homeworkers, working at home is not a temporary but a permanent way of working. The Finnish data clearly support one "truth": Homeworkers' income is low compared to the average income of their occupational group, especially among women. Moreover, social security benefits are often lacking.[21]

At least two factors account for the differences between the international discussion and the Finnish situation. Much research and debate elsewhere have focused on either the new trend of computer-based telework or, in the case of traditional homeworking, industrial piecework. As of the mid-1990s, distance work based on new technology is rather rare in Finland, whereas in the United States and many European countries routine data entry and word processing are more often commissioned as distance work. For this kind of labor, working conditions can be nearly as strict as those for industrial piecework, and the worker has very limited autonomy.

Research on such kinds of work will generate different results than investigation of homeworking as a whole. The problem with the discussion has been not the research results as such but the often-adopted habit of universalizing the results for certain kinds of homeworking and applying them to homeworking in general. Homeworking, thus, has been understood as a single phenomenon. However, the mapping out of the range of homeworking shows that home-based work exists on many levels with one factor in common: The work is done at home. This one factor is not enough to universalize the concepts of homeworking, its meanings, and its consequences.[22]

The dominant discussion associates the desirability of homeworking primarily with the nature of the work itself, its character and features, and with the worker's position in the labor market (how much in demand is her or his labor, and hence what are her or his chances of negotiating the terms and conditions of employment). My research on Finnish homeworkers shows that total life situation rather than character of work or position in the labor market determines experiences of homeworking.

The basic question, then, is: To what extent are people themselves able to form their life-totalities? This factor seems to be crucial in determining whether the experience of homeworking is predominantly positive or negative. The same things may be experienced positively by some people and negatively by others, but they may also be simultaneously both positive and negative for one and the same person. A clear example is the homeworker's chance of arranging her or his own working hours: This opportunity allows flexibility in time use but simultaneously creates the problem of extending work over the whole day and leads to the difficulty of separating work from leisure time. The total experience of such simultaneously valued and problematic characteristics of homeworking depends on the worker's life situation at each particular phase of her or his life. These characteristics may be either positive or negative regardless of, or at least not directly dependent on, the character of work. Instead, one's life-totality and one's chances of forming this totality influence the experience of homeworking.

Take the experience of homeworking as a form of production and the position of homeworkers in the labor market. If homeworking has a clear market of its own outside which the homeworking women cannot move (because of the structure of the labor force, or because of their life situations, or because of their husbands' or their own values), then the economic situation of homeworkers suffers and a little flexibility in everyday life will not make it much better. But the situation of such a homeworker can also contain other ramifications. Ulla, who has a monotonous piecework job, changed her workplace to the home from the factory when her children were small. She has continued to work at home and plans to do so even in the future because she has more say about the course of her day. Her experience resembles that of a knitter in the United States who explained, "Working in a factory is demeaning, and working at home has dignity."[23]

Although homeworking is not always a clear-cut choice, individual suitability enters into the decision. My available data do not tell us how many people may have started working at home but later quit because they could not adjust. It is possible that people either can or cannot work at home, as with shift work, and that those who do not adjust quit if they can. Until the economic crisis of the early 1990s, women in Finland had alternative ways to earn wages.

The data presented here describe the situation in 1985–1986. Since then, the economic situation in Finland—as throughout Europe, the United States, and Canada—has changed dramatically. The economic downturn has probably led to changes in the structure of homeworking in Finland. Nowhere has homeworking become as common as was predicted in the 1980s, neither in the utopian version, à la Toffler, nor in the dystopian one, in which teleworkers would replace 40 percent of clerical office workers. However, we do not yet know the consequences of the Western European economic recession and the subsequent restructuring of the political economy.

In Finland, the recession has reduced home-based work in many fields, such as fur farms or consulting and public relations firms, but it may be extending it in others, such as the textile industry. Because there is no generalized form of homeworking, economic development will have various impacts on different fields. There has been little public discussion about homeworking in Finland in the 1990s, but labor ministries have shown interest in homeworking as one form of "flexible work organization," and this idea might lead to more activity because of the need to restructure the economy. There is also interest in developing home-based work and telework as a strategy to keep rural areas and the archipelago populated and economically viable. Development projects have begun both in traditional homeworking, such as knitting, and in telework.

We have seen that Finnish women have a long tradition in the labor market. In the mid-1990s, the self-evident right of women to paid employment has come under attack because of the recession and restructuring of the economy. What might happen if the structures that have made homeworking in Finland "a different case" start to fail? Cuts in the public sector, especially in social services, endanger women's jobs because the majority of the public-sector employees are women. The cuts also threaten women's right to employment because municipal governments have targeted the day care system for fiscal cuts. Even in Nordic countries, with their equality-based model of gender relations, it is quite possible for conservatives to use a recession as a reason for demanding that women move back home to take care of their children and old people. European integration may put additional pressure on women's employment by generating competition for work in the service sector between Finnish women and less trained workers from other European countries.

The recession is not the only reason for the downsizing of the welfare state. Libertarian voices ask people "to take more responsibility for each other" and demand more private competition in social services. That the people who would "take responsibility" would be women; that private competition is perhaps not the best way to care for children, the sick, and the elderly is not a consideration in this kind of thinking, which is presented as "a new alternative."

Amid all the talk of the free European market, adaptation to a new market situation, and restructuring of the economy, we also hear more and more voices raised in support of "flexible" production and "flexible" use of labor. These notions include first, part-time work; second, periodic and casual work; and third, home-based work. The first two concepts have meant, at least in Finland, flexibility for employers. Part-time work has been uncommon in Finland, unlike other Nordic countries. Unlike other Nordic women, Finnish women have not wanted or not been able to choose part-time work as a solution to the problem of combining employment and child care. Now both periodic and part-time work, and the periodic and casual employment of women in particular, has become more common. Whether the same will happen with homeworking remains to be seen.

Notes

1 Sheila Allen and Carol Wolkowitz, *Homeworking: Myths and Realities* (London: Macmillan, 1987); Liz Bisset and Ursula Huws, *Sweated Labour: Homeworking in Britain Today* (Nottingham: Low Pay Unit, 1985); Monica Elling, *På tröskeln till ett nytt liv?* (On the threshold to a new life?)(Göteborg: Arbetslivscentrum, 1984); Monica Elling and Marianne Parmsund, *Långt borta och nära: Om distansarbete på kontorsområdet* (Far away and nearby: On distance work in office work) (Göteborg: Arbetslivscentrum, 1982); Ursula Huws, *The New Homeworkers: New Technology and the Changing Location of White-Collar Work* (Nottingham: Low Pay Unit, 1984); Merete Lie, "Fjernarbeid, likestilling og 'det gode liv'?" (Distance work, equality and 'good life'?) *Plan og Arbeid* 5–6 (1984): 2–7; Merete Lie in collboration with Ann-Jorun Berg, Elin Kvande, and Eli Kvåle, *Lønnet hjemmearbeid* (Paid labor at home)(Trondheim: Institutt for industriell miljøforskning, 1978); Margrethe H. Olson, "Remote Office Work: Changing Patterns in Space and Time," *Communications of the ACM* 26, 3 (1983): 182–187; Margrethe H. Olson, "New Information Technology and Organizational Culture," *MIS Quarterly*, special issue (1982): 71–92; Gitte Vedel, *Just Pick Up a Telephone! Remote Office Work in Sweden* (Copenhagen: The Copenhagen School of Economics and Business Administration, Information Systems Research Group, 1984); and Gitte Vedel, Ewa Gunnarsson, and Sanne Ipsen, *Hjemme godt, men ude bedst? Distancearbejde i Frankrig* (At home is well but out is best? Distance work in France)(Roskilde: Roskilde Universitetsforlag, 1983).

2 Although the sample is rather small, it is representative. The structure of the survey material corresponds fairly well to that of the total population of homeworkers in regard to numbers, structure of occupations and occupational status, type of work, education, and gender division. I collected the homeworkers sample in connection with the living conditions sample because it became clear only later that homeworkers actually could be picked out from the population census. However, the living conditions survey also made it possible to create a rich database on homeworkers.

3 Multiple classification analysis (MCA) is a type of analysis in which you can look simultaneously at multiple variables to explain one variable. The explaining variables can be both quantitative and qualitative. One can measure the relative "explaining power" of the hypothesized explaining variables to see which of them is the most important in explaining the variance of the issue in question. For more on MCA, see J. A. Sonqvist, *Multivariate Model Building: The Validation of a Search Strategy* (Ann Arbor: Institute for Social Research, University of Michigan, 1971).

4 This kind of story building on the basis of quantitative data was only possible because of the many-sided data.

5 Catherine Hakim, *Home-Based Work in Britain: A Report on the 1981 National Homeworking Survey and the DE Research Programme on Homework*, Research Paper No. 60 (London: Department of Employment, 1987); Catherine Hakim, *Employers' Use of Outwork: A Study Using the 1980 Workplace Industrial Relations Survey and the*

1981 National Survey of Homeworking, Research Paper No. 44 (London: Department of Employment, 1985); Catherine Hakim and Roger Dennis, *Homeworking in Wages Council Industries: A Study Based on Wages Inspectorate Records of Pay and Earnings*, Research Paper No. 37 (London: Department of Employment, 1982).

6 Lewis A. Coser and Rose Laub Coser, "The Housewife and Her 'Greedy Family,'" in *Greedy Institutions: Patterns of Undivided Commitment*, ed. Lewis A. Coser (New York: The Free Press, 1974), p. 91. On homeworkers in family firms, see also Kathleen Christensen, *Women and Home-Based Work: The Unspoken Contract* (New York: Henry Holt and Company, 1988), pp. 69–105.

7 Lie et al., *Lønnet hjemmearbeid*; Bisset and Huws, *Sweated Labour*; Huws, *The New Homeworkers*; Allen and Wolkowitz, *Homeworking*, and Christensen, *Women and Home-Based Work*. Where research has shown that women are not the overwhelming majority of homeworkers, the results have been presented with astonishment, as in Tom Forester, *High-Tech Society: The Story of the Information Technology Revolution* (Oxford: Basil Blackwell, 1987), p. 162.

8 Gillian Pugh, "Reconciling Employment and Caring for Very Young Children in United Kingdom," *Report from the Conference "Parental Employment and Caring for Children: Policies and Services in EC and Nordic Countries"* (Copenhagen: Socialministeriet, 1993), p. 133; Figure 3–13, "Employment," in *The American Woman, 1994–95: Where We Stand*, eds. Cynthia Costello and Anne J. Stone (New York: Norton, 1994), p. 302.

9 Anna-Maija Lehto, *Työelämän laatu ja tasa-arvo* (Quality of working life and equality)(Helsinki: Tilastokeskus, tutkimuksia 189, 1991), p. 40; Table 3–7, "Employment," in *The American Woman*, p. 291.

10 Harriet Strandell, "Kolmen naissukupolven kokemuksia työstä ja perheestä" (Three generations of women tell about their experiences of work and family), in *Perhe, työ ja tunteet* (Family, work, and emotions), eds. Elina Haavio-Mannila, Riitta Jallinoja, and Harriet Strandell (Helsinki: WSOY, 1984), pp. 203–294.

11 On the position of women and the building up of the Finnish welfare state, see Anneli Anttonen, Lea Henriksson and Ritva Natkin, eds., *Naisten hyvinvointivaltio* (Women's welfare state), (Tampere: Vastapaino, 1994); Raija Julkunen, *Hyvinvointivaltio käännekohdassa* (The welfare state at a turning point)(Tampere: Vastapaino, 1992); and Tuula Heiskanen and Liisa Rantalaiho, eds., *Gendered Practices in Working Life* (London: Macmillan, forthcoming).

12 Since 1985, the leave has been called parental leave because the parents can divide the period of caretaking. The mother has to take the first 105 days of the parental leave, but either parent can use the rest. In addition, and connected to the birth, the father can take a six- to twelve-day paternity leave, and on top of this, since 1991 the father can take a further six days' leave whenever it suits the family during the parental leave period.

13 See Edmund Dahlström, "Everyday-Life Theories and Their Historical and Ideological Contexts," in *The Multiparadigmatic Trend in Sociology*, ed. Ulf Himmelstrand (Uppsala: Almqvist and Wiksell, 1987), pp. 93–114.

14 On the time structures of everyday life in general and of homeworkers in particular, see Minna Salmi, "Autonomy and Time-Use in Everyday Life: The Case of Home-Based Work," in *Gendered Practices in Working Life.*

15 Christensen, *Women and Home-Based Work,* p. 13.

16 I have put the words *creative* and *routine* in quotation marks to point out that such definitions of the type of work are diffuse and problematic. Most work includes both creative and routine tasks.

17 Tom Forester, "The Myth of the Electronic Cottage," *Futures* 3 (June 1988): 232.

18 Alvin Toffler, *The Third Wave* (New York: William Morrow and Company, 1980).

19 See Karen Davies, *Women and Time: Weaving the Strands of Everyday Life* (Lund: Grahns boktryckeri, 1989); and Tora Friberg, *Kvinnors vardag: Om kvinnors arbete och liv. Anpassningsstrategier i tid och rum* (Women's everyday: On women's work and life. Coping strategies in time and space)(Lund: Lund University Press, 1990), pp. 127–128.

20 Work has been classified as "creative" or "routine" according to the grade of autonomy in work. The grade of autonomy can be seen as a continuum on which the autonomy is highest if one controls decisions on the end product of one's work, the working methods, the working order and timetables. The grade of autonomy is lowest if the worker can decide only when she or he works, and not what she or he is doing and how she or he is doing it.

21 The lack of social security compared to regular employment is connected partly with the entrepreneur status of many homeworkers and partly with the fact that even homeworkers who work regularly for the same employer often do not have the same status and benefits as regular employees but are considered free-lancers whose position is like that of entrepreneurs. Entrepreneurs have to pay for their old-age pension and unemployment insurance themselves according to their earnings, and if the earnings are small, the payments remain small. Many are apparently less than eager to make these payments at all.

22 See Belinda Probert and Judy Wajcman, "Bringing It All Back Home: A Study of New Technology Homework," Paper presented to the British Sociological Association Conference, Edinburgh, March 1988, p. 5; Robin Leidner, "Home Work: A Study in the Interaction of Work and Family Organization," in *Research in the Sociology of Work: A Research Annual—High Tech Work*, vol. 4, eds. Richard L. Simpson and Ida Harper Simpson (London: JAI Press Inc., 1988), pp. 69–94; R. E. Pahl, "Homeworking: Myths and Realities," *Contemporary Sociology* 5 (1989): 716–717; and Harriet Presser and Elizabeth Bamberger, "American Women Who Work at Home for Pay: Distinctions and Determinants," *Social Science Quarterly* (December 1993): 815–837.

23 Eileen Boris, "Homework and Women's Rights: The Case of the Vermont Knitters, 1980–1985," *Signs* 13 (Autumn 1987): 111.

Mrs. Tony Totaro, husband—a cement laborer with irregular work—and their two children. She makes $2–$2.50 a week on lace. She confesses to the photographer Lewis Hine: "I'd rather work for a factory. They pay more."

Integrating living and working space. This family in Zapotlanejo, Mexico, converted its garage into a store. When the business grew and needed to expand, family members removed the wall that separated the garage from the living room.

Separating work and living space. A male homeworker sewing in Zapotlanejo, Mexico.

Homework is common in the garment industry in countries around the world. Seamstresses assemble pre-cut materials for subcontractors.

Seamstress in Nezahualcóyotl, Mexico.

Seamstress in Nova Iguaçu,
Rio de Janeiro.

Seamstresses

Seamstress in Bangkok, Thailand.

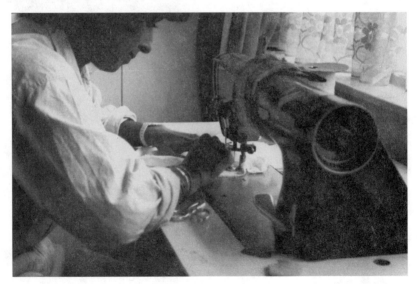

Seamstress in West Yorkshire, Britain.

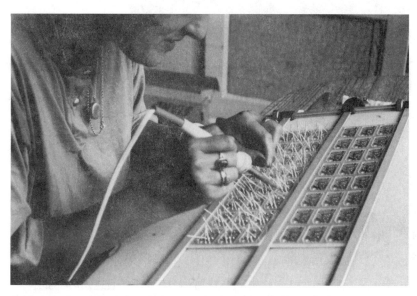

Soldering printed circuit boards: homeworker in West Yorkshire, Britain.

Child minder in Finland serves breakfast, a warm lunch and a snack to children during the day. Here Pirkko sits at her kitchen table with Mats (4 yrs.), brothers Julius (4 yrs.) and Jonas (6 yrs.), and little Janina (2 yrs.) having the afternoon snack.

Batik workers in Yogyakarta, Indonesia, work under the putting-out system. Batik making involves tedious tracing of designs, waxing and dyeing.

Preparing samosas for sale in Rang Mahal, the Walled City of Lahore, Pakistan.

Headquarters of the International Labor Organization in Geneva, Switzerland. ILO projects seek to improve the rights, wages, and working conditions of homeworkers, and international debates on homework take place under the umbrella of the ILO.

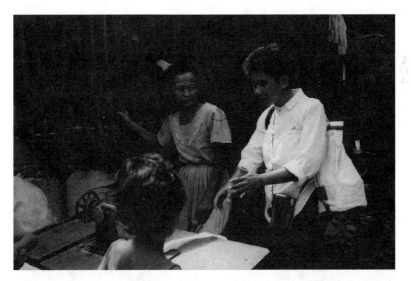

Support from the ILO's project on Rural Women Homeworkers in the New Putting-Out System helped establish PATAMABA, the national network of homeworkers in the Philippines. Ka Mimi Acosta, a PATAMABA organizer, talks to seamstresses in Viscayas.

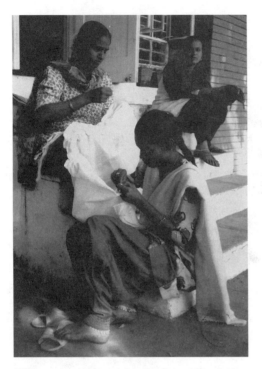

SEWA coop members, doing tie-dye, on the steps
of SEWA Reception Center in Ahmedabad, India.

International Homeworking Conference held in Bradford, U.K., in July 1992.
Participants from SEWA and the Netherlands speak to the meeting.

Homeworkers from West Yorkshire take part in a lobby of the House of Commons, with Members of Parliament, October, 1991.

Homeworkers march to Eaton Center, Toronto's largest shopping center, to protest low wages and launch the Clean Clothes Campaign, November 1992.

Part Three »

« Divergent Responses

State Policies and
Homeworker Organizing

10

Making Cadillacs and Buicks
for General Motors

Homework as Rural Development
in the Midwestern United States

« *Christina Gringeri*

> We build Buicks here [at home].... We're building Cadillacs
> and Buicks and Chryslers and Fords.
>
> —Midwestern homeworker, 1988

INDUSTRIAL HOMEWORK IN RURAL AREAS OF THE UNITED STATES HIGHLIGHTS two intersecting issues: the role of the state in economic restructuring and industrial relocation, and the importance of women as workers in restructured production and local development.[1] The ways in which these issues intersect are clearly illustrated in this case study of Prairie Hills, Iowa, and Riverton, Wisconsin, two rural communities that recruited employers of homeworkers as part of their local development strategies.[2] The states supported and financed homeworking as development and, in doing so, supported the fragmentation and relocation of some parts of automotive assembly production. In the social context of these rural communities, development officials and local leaders defined the homeworking jobs as "secondary," part-time employment that provided "supplemental" income and often perceived them as women's work.

Local leaders in these communities came to see home-based assembly work as a viable development strategy because the agricultural and manufacturing economies faltered seriously in the early 1980s. Land values and commodity prices declined, leaving farm operators with higher debt loads and decreased means to pay those debts, resulting in increases in insolvency among farming families. Manufacturing jobs declined, plants stood empty, and unemployment rates increased. Local retail sectors also felt the decline as purchasing power decreased.[3] In this context, any job development seemed a step in the right direction to the local development corporations in Prairie Hills and Riverton.

The Middle Company (TMC), a Fortune 500 manufacturer and subcontractor of General Motors (GM) was ready to step into this rural context. Midlevel managers and engineers from TMC had persuaded GM that portions of the automotive assembly process could be accomplished more cost effectively by rural people working at home than in the factory. In 1986, TMC went to Prairie Hills and established the first warehouse to distribute automotive parts to homeworkers; its success in Prairie Hills motivated the company to establish a second warehouse in Riverton.[4] The process of such development is important in understanding the relationships between TMC, the workers, and the local governments and aids in clarifying the role of the state in restructured production.

However, it is the process and organization of production as viewed from the workers' households that forms the basis for understanding the centrality of gender and the household division of labor to homeworking. As sociologist Enzo Mingione has pointed out, the nature of informal sector work is most accurately observed and understood at the "local" level because the local social and historical context actively influences the way informal production develops, and these factors contribute to a great deal of local variation.[5] This point is especially true for homework because the performance of paid work in the home transforms the organization of both paid and unpaid work activities.

Thus, the household, as the locus of production and reproduction, becomes the window through which to view paid and unpaid work in the home and to discuss the relationship between the state, TMC, and the homeworkers. The context of the local communities becomes the means to examine the process of a development strategy that incorporated informal-sector jobs and to discuss the ways in which local development strategies are built upon gendered notions of women's work.

Methods

This essay draws on ethnographic field research done in two rural Midwestern communities during 1988 and 1989. I conducted in-depth personal interviews with three development officials and two elected officials in both Prairie Hills and Riverton and with a total of seventy-five homeworkers from the two locations. In each community, a group of three development officials had formed a private development corporation comprised of a prominent businessman, a banker, and a lawyer. In Riverton, the businessman chaired the corporation, and in Prairie Hills, the banker served as head. I also analyzed documents such as minutes from meetings, grant applications, project files, and newspaper articles.[6]

The Process of Rural Development

TMC is based in the Midwest. It manufactures various industrial and automotive components, including metal fasteners, plastic carriers, measuring tools, and other precision equipment. As of 1986, TMC was described as employing roughly eight thousand people worldwide in twenty-five domestic and twenty foreign plants, all of which were nonunion shops. In the mid-1980s, TMC began to look for rural sites in the Midwest in which to develop smaller plants, making a concerted and successful effort to move jobs from a single location in an urban setting to several locations in smaller cities and towns. Wisconsin used state subsidies to attract six of these smaller factories to several rural communities over five years. The mayor of Riverton spoke directly about the motivations behind industrial relocations: "A lotta these companies chose to come out to the rural areas because they felt they could get by with paying lower wages, which they did…. And of course, the companies came out here to get away from the unions and the union wages. I understood that the companies were in a crunch because of offshore competitiveness…. [This company believes] they can carry on a good enough relationship with their employees, that they don't need unions…. They said the fastest way that they'd pull out of Riverton would be if they unionized. [The manager] told me in no uncertain terms they were not antiunion, they were pro-people." Avoiding unions figures prominently in local officials' understanding of what motivates industrial relocations. At the same time that these relocations were occurring, TMC was developing the cottage industry plan.[7] It was successful in redesigning the assembly process of a variety of small auto parts so that the subcomponents could be shipped to rural families for assembly and then returned to GM for final assembly on cars and trucks.

The cottage industry concept served two major company interests. It fragmented the process of production then in use at the GM factory in Detroit so that production could be removed from the factory. Decentralization of production made it easier to relocate to a lower wage, nonunion area. When the reorganization of the work process was completed, two managers from TMC went to Prairie Hills and later to Riverton to look for sites and local financing. The two managers were quite frank about how they selected the sites for homeworking. Economic conditions and the need for work figured prominently in their comparisons of different communities: "The northern community had a very professional development team, but the area was too prosperous and didn't seem to us to need homeworking enough to support the operation. The soil was very black, the land flat for miles, the homes recently sided, and there was new model farm equipment. There just wouldn't be enough demand for the work. Then we went to Prairie Hills, and they have an aggressive development team there, too. But Prairie Hills is built on rolling hills, it's full of red and yellow clay, has lower bushel-per-acre yields, smaller homes, less recent farm machinery. We knew the demand for work was there, and we were right."[8]

In each community, there was a development group of three men actively involved in recruiting TMC and developing homeworking jobs. The state-level Departments of Development introduced managers from TMC to the development corporation officers of each community. In each group, the banker and the prominent businessman were the most active members; because the groups were formed as private corporations, no elected officials were members. However, the local mayors were influential in their support of this development strategy.

The local development officials expressed their main interests as general economic improvement and community survival. The bankers and the businessmen had personal economic stakes in their communities; farm insolvency and retail bankruptcy made for tough times in business and banking, too. One homeworker observed, "The bank's the one that told the city, ya know, 'Hey, we put this building up. We can get this industry to come to town, and they'll help a lotta people out in this community. They'll get jobs and....' They don't tell them, 'They'll be helping us [the bank] out, because we got a lotta people out there that aren't gonna get their notes paid if we don't help 'em out.' And so they was lookin' out for their own interest." Homeworking as development was a fairly inexpensive way to increase household income and perhaps local purchasing power while strengthening the local private sector.

In Prairie Hills, the banker-developer handled initial recruitment of homeworkers, leading to local criticism that the newly created jobs were going only to insolvent farmers. One of the first homeworkers in Prairie Hills recalled: "One lady said to me, well, something about, well, 'Is your farm gonna be sold? Or, are you guys, when is your bankruptcy coming up?' We said, 'What?' And she said, 'Well, all of us are, and were recommended by the bank because we're totally broke.' ...And I did notice right away that the way they were talking, it was all farmers that were hurting really bad." In fact, nine out of the first ten home-based contractors did qualify for displaced worker subsidies for job training, lending support to community members' perceptions of who was getting hired. Handing out jobs during a time of economic distress also served to buttress social status and local power for the banker in Prairie Hills. Access to the jobs in Riverton depended more on one's persistence and one's connection to the local TMC manager, a young displaced farmer, than on one's lack of financial viability.

The development officials in these communities believed that homeworking was a good opportunity for economic reasons. Homeworking could offset agricultural decline and loss of retail business, while increasing cash flow in households struggling to make ends meet. Prairie Hills applied for state funds, claiming "dire need" for this project "to maintain our county seat town, and give our townspeople additional income for their physical and mental stability." Furthermore, wrote one development official in support of the grant application, "We feel the impact of this new business will place the dollars of income in the hands of our financially strapped citizens and area farmers. We need the financial assistance that a project like this will provide.... This would increase tax rolls at both county and state levels. There would be less unemployment paid in the state. It would take some off unemployment and not allow additional recipients."[9] A Riverton development official said the local development committee was very receptive to the cottage industry idea because "it was only for farmers, because they were the people that seemed to be most traumatized at the time.... If we could get some cash flow back into the hands of these farmers, the businesses in town were going to be better off, too." The cottage industry concept made economic sense to local officials, who saw job creation simply as increasing the cash flow in households, resulting in a stronger local private sector.

However, the financing of homework in these two communities shows a pattern of each community and state bearing the costs and risks involved in supporting new industry. TMC generally bore little or no risk because most of its capital investment was in small machinery and inventory that could easily be moved if necessary. Both communities absorbed the costs of purchasing property and developing it for industry as well as the costs of warehouse construction. TMC leased the warehouses and was not responsible for them after its occupancy. As one local development official put it, "The industry is not at risk whatsoever other than their lease." TMC entered each community without having invested initially in property or development and could leave without the financial burden of property ownership. The initial risks and costs of industrial development were largely borne by the states and towns, which, concluded one official, "decreases the cost to make it more appealing to the industry."

Defining the homeworkers as independent contractors also decreased the costs of labor for TMC. The Internal Revenue Service (IRS) uses four main criteria to determine whether an individual is an independent contractor. First, the individual must be free to control a substantial part of his or her business life. Workers must be able to set the deadlines on their work; have control over negotiating salary, wages, or other compensation, including benefits; and be responsible for furnishing the equipment and materials necessary for the job. However, in this case, the homeworkers are subject to deadlines imposed by TMC, cannot negotiate the piece rate, and sign a lease for equipment provided by TMC.

Second, the opportunity for profit or loss must exist in the business venture. An independent contractor is in control of the major factors that determine profit or loss, such as price, location, advertising, and volume. The homeworkers clearly lack control over any of these factors. TMC controls the piece rate for the assembly work, the location of the warehouses, and the quantity and availability of work.

Capital investment is the third criterion for determination of employment status. An independent contractor is one who has risk capital invested in the business, but the homeworkers lack entrepreneurial risk in the assembly business. If TMC should declare bankruptcy, the homeworkers would be laid off but would not suffer loss as a result of any investment in TMC as an enterprise. Another way of assessing this risk factor is to determine whether the worker has a proprietary interest in the firm and is able to sell or give away such interest; if so, the individual is an independent contractor. Although homeworkers informally share their subcontracted work with others, they are not able to sell or give away the contract itself.

The fourth criterion of an independent contractor is the ability to terminate the contract with the firm and move the operation to a new location. Clearly, only TMC has this ability to locate the assembly operation where it chooses and, as such, might be considered an independent contractor for GM. For independent contractors, the ability to terminate the contract must rest with them rather than with the employing unit. In the case of TMC, a contract may be terminated by the company as well as by the worker.

Homeworkers, then, are in reality disguised wage workers for TMC rather than independent contractors.[10] This distinction is important for the purposes of compensation, insurance, and taxes. It is also central to a discussion of how TMC shares or distributes the risks and costs of labor. By defining the workers as independent contractors, TMC writes into the contract that they "shall not be eligible for any employee benefits." TMC is able to avoid paying for benefits such as health and life insurance or pension plans, realizing major savings. Additionally, TMC is able to avoid paying unemployment tax and does not contribute to workers' compensation or disability insurance.

Social Security contributions, however, blur the distinction between the employee and the self-employed. At the outset, TMC did not deduct anything from the homeworkers' pay in Prairie Hills. Several months later, on advice of its lawyers, TMC changed its policy and began deducting the employee portion of Social Security from the homeworkers' checks. But they lowered the piece rates to pay for the employer portion so that workers actually earned less than before the deductions for Social Security. One homeworker explained, "Well, like we were getting four cents per bolt, and they lowered it to 3.8 cents." Although on paper the company appeared to be contributing to Social Security and treating the homeworkers as employees, in reality the workers were paying the equivalent of the self-employed rate into Social Security. Because of the lowering of the piece rate another homeworker could feel that, "We've contributed our half, but they haven't contributed their half as far as Social Security goes." In Riverton, TMC simply deducted the self-employed amount from the workers' checks, a contradictory practice because the self-employed are responsible for paying Social Security on their own.

The blurring of labor status affects another important area: the deduction of work-related expenses from income taxes. As self-employed workers, or independent contractors, the homeworkers should be able to deduct work-related expenses such as gas, mileage, electricity, and the cost of the work space. Homeworkers who operated farms simply took most of these deductions as farm-related business expenses, but rural nonfarm residents found that unless they owned a business, there was no way to deduct expenses related to homeworking. One worker pointed out:

> They withhold Social Security. Just enough that we can't do anything with it at the end of a year. I was kind of hoping that come tax time, we could maybe turn some of our utilities that we use down there, a percentage of our utilities over, because we use an air compressor, a heater, a fan, and our lights. And that, you know, pulls juice. But we can't do it.... Because they don't consider it self-employed; as long as they are holding Social Security out, then we are working for them, basically. Now this is what our tax man told us, just the other night.... Our tax man told us that the first year that TMC came into town, they didn't withhold anything, not Social Security or anything, so the people could deduct like their utilities, or if they had to set up a special place to do it, you know, they could use some of that for deduction.

In terms of tax regulations related to labor status, these homeworkers do not experience the advantages of independent employment. They absorb many work-related costs as homeworkers, yet they cannot deduct any of the expenses. Although the IRS considers them employees, TMC does not contribute to any social insurance other than Social Security as if they were employees.

This situation is clearly another aspect of "decreasing the costs to make it more appealing to industry."

Labor status as an independent contractor rather than as an employee contributes to the definition of these jobs as secondary and of the income as supplemental. If these assembly jobs were defined as employee positions and offered some benefits and stability, they would be closer to the idea of a "primary job," which would usually employ more men than women. This difference is illustrated clearly in the employment patterns of local factories, where men held the more stable and better-compensated assembly jobs. In one small factory, the only female employee was the receptionist. Status as a contractor allows TMC to organize production in a cheaper manner, which is acceptable within the confines of a "secondary" job fit for women workers.

Defining the homeworkers as independent contractors when the labor relations and process of production indicate that they are actually employees allows TMC to pass risks and costs on to the workers. The pattern that is observed at the community level, with TMC setting up at little or no risk to the firm, is the same with respect to the workers. The workers bear the risks of self-employment, such as occasional work stoppages and responsibility for unemployment, with none of the benefits of independence, such as control over the labor process, the wages, or the investment of profits. They are subject to the control of the company as though they were employees, but they share none of the employee's benefits, such as guarantees of minimum wages and maximum hours. In the same way that the communities subsidized and supported TMC's local development at greater risk to themselves than to the company, the workers subsidize TMC's production with greater benefits and savings to the company than to themselves because they are not classified as employees. Because the state, represented by local capital and development officials, approves and subsidizes the development of jobs in which workers also subsidize the labor process, it acts as a "conduit" for the interests of TMC. That is, the state indirectly passes costs and risks on to workers by financing homeworking as job creation under these conditions. The relationships between TMC, the states, and the workers are such that TMC passes costs on to workers and the communities, and the state also indirectly passes costs on to workers.

Women's Work as Development: Supplemental Income and Secondary Employment

Women as workers absorb many of these labor-related costs. Development officials were just as clear about the "who" of homeworking as they were about the "why." At first, said a Riverton official, "we were not real excited" about the cottage industry work, mostly because TMC was not going to pay any benefits. But then the development committee members "talked to some of the people that were interested in that type of work, and they thought it was wonderful. They just wanted to jump at the chance. [Who?] ... Well, the women that are doing it. The farm wives that don't have to hire babysitters, they don't have to leave their homes every day." Another local official agreed that although the jobs paid no benefits, "that wasn't what the people needed at this time. What they needed was cash flow." This elected official described the ideal homeworker: "The farm wives that take an active part in their farming operation, when they weren't there [because of off-farm jobs], it was having a bad impact on the farming operations, and it was separating families and creating just bad human-type emotion. And so this way, they could take the work home, be with their kids, be on the farm, rainy days both husband and wife would work on 'em, and, y'know, it was bringing families that were getting separated together."

In keeping with local norms and values, the elected officials and local developers speak of a farm crisis, about the farmers (men) being traumatized, and of the need to increase cash flow. In the same breath, the officials and developers speak of the solution as employing farmers' wives. Homeworking was strongly gender typed in the perceptions of development officials and workers. In "desperate" times or "rainy days," men might help with women's work, but women were the workers. Off-farm work as a survival strategy during and after the farm crisis relies heavily on women as wage laborers.

Local developers pictured women as the homeworkers and, indeed, women were the majority of the assemblers. Both communities clearly portray homework as "women's work" largely because the work is done at home, which is seen as women's sphere; the wages earned are low and are defined as supplemental or secondary income. Popular perceptions of the advantages of homeworking are often tied to responsibilities defined as primarily female. These perceptions of homework were common among workers and their families as well as among the developers and elected officials.

Homework was more commonly typed as women's work in Riverton, where the workers were assembling small screws and washers; many men in the community and in the homeworking households expressed the opinion that women, with their "small, dexterous" hands, were much faster at assembling the screws than were men. The bolts and grommets that make up suspension pieces are much larger and heavier; hence, there was more male participation in the homework in Prairie Hills. Interestingly, whenever power tools were used in the assembly process in either community, men were more likely to participate and to be those using the tools. TMC contracts with one individual per household, regardless of who actually performs the assembly work. A contractor list showed several men as homeworkers, but in reality, women were most frequently the workers responsible for the completed work. In many households, adults and children shared the work and sometimes sub-contracted it out to neighbors.

In all households except one, assembly homeworking was one aspect of multiple income earning. Farm-operating households tended to have one main full-time job off the farm, held by either adult; rural nonfarm households tended to combine a variety of part-time jobs and perhaps one full-time paying job outside the home.[11] One household, a highly indebted dairy farm, lived on the income from homeworking for several months per year; the monthly income was low enough to qualify this and a few other households for a number of public assistance programs in health and nutrition. One homeworker observed that the first groups of contractors were "families that couldn't even buy groceries, that were really destitute for some income, those were the ones they tried to pick first."

Local development officials frequently described home-based assembly jobs as "supplemental" and "secondary." *Supplemental income* was also an important term to TMC managers, who stressed to the community and the homeworkers that the assembly work was meant only to supplement, rather than provide, a living wage. One homeworker said TMC had given her the strong impression that the work "really is part time, and don't count on much." Another homeworker said TMC informed her that the work was intended to provide "part-time extra income."

Over time, the homeworkers realized that the income was called supplemental not only because the pay was low but because the work was unstable. One homeworker discussed her sense of frustration and exploitation:

> Well, it's the irritation of people, big business using people, because sometimes you had a kit.[12] When you started out it was a part-time job. Just like thirty-eight to forty hours, forty weeks a year, is what they originally told us. Then after a while, they said, well, it's gonna be about full-time. All you can do. Then two weeks later, you don't have a kit. And it's the frustration, I guess, of not knowing. You know, sometimes you depend upon, and I know we're warned. Don't depend on these. Don't depend upon the check. But you know, so you think every week you're going to have a kit. And then, all of a sudden, you never know until you drive in that day whether or not you're going to have a kit the next week.

In the view of local development officials, the TMC homeworking jobs were secondary jobs, the income definitely supplemental. One official said, "It was another form of employment. It was never mentioned or introduced in this community as being a form of primary employment. I don't think that that type of labor is a primary employer. I don't know anybody that could live on that. It was intended as a supplemental employment.... The intent being that it was not intended to take the place of primary employment." Secondary employment, continued this official, is "low-paying employment." Once they knew TMC wanted to establish a warehouse, the local development officials informally surveyed local women, especially farm women, to see if there was enough interest to support the industry. Homeworking was the kind of job one took to provide a second income in a household, and, observed one committee member, a second income is "what buys a lot of the frills and the goodies, you know, of a family. That the wife comes in with her paycheck and buys the new furniture or buys new carpeting, the new dress, or food, or something that isn't an absolute necessity. It's that extra income coming in." These new jobs created under the auspices of economic development were clearly seen as being performed by women and as providing supplemental income that "added to the family kitty" but did not take the place of "primary employment." This notion contrasts, however, with the "dire need" that community officials expressed in recruiting the homeworking jobs to their locales and in acquiring state financing for TMC. "Buying a lot of frills" also contrasts with the experience of homeworkers who depended on the income, at times, for necessities. One homeworking couple said, "We use it to buy groceries and the essentials. You know, that's all we had." The farmers and unemployed men were perceived as being in "dire need," but the development strategy incorporated women as low-wage workers in secondary employment to supplement household cash needs. This dichotomy between perception and practice underscores the point that informal sector work can be an inexpensive way of increasing purchasing power to strengthen the local private sector.

In approving TMC's cottage industry jobs as development, the local communities shouldered the responsibility of procuring funds to subsidize new industrial plants. Decentralization of funding for development in Prairie Hills and Riverton supported the creation of particular jobs that, from the outset, were defined as advantageous for women. In contrast, men in both communities filled other jobs created with local and state subsidies, both by TMC and by other firms, which required training and offered better pay and advancement. In fact, one development official and local businessman described a TMC machining plant as "the first primary employment" in this community in over thirty years. This TMC plant is "predominately male" because "it's heavy work, hard work. Noisy, terrible noisy. Women can't talk when they're working." The use of Jobs Training Partnership Act (JTPA)[13] funds to train the local manager of the TMC warehouse is another example of public financing of a stable, relatively well-paying or primary job, which is then seen as a man's job. Furthermore, Prairie Hills used JTPA funds allocated for "displaced or disadvantaged" workers for pre-employment training of contractors nine out of ten of whom were male, even though women in these households did the assembly work. Decentralized job-training funds can be used as local officials "see fit" as long as individuals meet eligibility criteria. In practice this idea can mean, as it did in Prairie Hills and Riverton, that communities use the funds to retrain men for "primary employment" and channel women into "secondary" and "supplemental" jobs.

Decentralization enhances local autonomy. It allows officials in local government and managers of capital to subsidize development and job creation in ways that seem congruent with their own and others' values. Decentralization of the development process allows the process to be infused with the norms and values both of the local communities and of the relocating firm. In this case, the communities and TMC infused the process of development with traditional notions that women's primary responsibilities are home and family and that paid work is a secondary responsibility. Under this ideology, it appears natural that women fill slots for low-paid, less stable work. Such work reinforces the definition of women's primary responsibilities and, in effect, reproduces traditional gender roles. Development, or homeworking job creation in these two communities, supports the reproduction of gender roles, which maintains and reproduces the labor supply for those jobs as well as for similar kinds of jobs.[14]

This link between development and the role of gender points to the importance of, and interaction between, the local state and the household in regulating both labor and development. Decentralization in the process of development allows for less state regulation of development and job creation, and decreased regulation of homeworking opens the door to greater regulation of work through community and family relations. The next sections explore two themes—the process and organization of production and the meaning of flexibility—that highlight ways in which homework as paid work interacts with unpaid work in the context of the household.

Process and Organization of Production

Household composition shapes participation in the homework process. The completion of the work each week depends on who participates for how long, the schedule of activities that week, and a number of other considerations that vary among households as well as among household members. The general pattern is that each contracting household usually has one person, not necessarily the person named on the contract, who takes responsibility for completing the work. The responsible person may actually do most of the work, or that person may delegate the work and make sure it gets done. When the responsible person is an adult woman, the assembly work is accomplished along with housework, child care, farm work, and sometimes another outside paid job. Most of the adult males responsible for homework combined it with farming and tended to delegate more of it to other persons.

Most households share the homework, although the extent of such sharing varies tremendously. Where the adult woman is responsible for the work, it is largely children who supplement her labor, either through household chores or home assembly. Some parents pay children a nominal amount, along the same lines as an allowance. Older children, such as teenagers, usually receive more: They tend to do more assembly work more regularly, so the family may treat it as an outside job for wages. Generally, children in homeworking families in both areas put in very few hours, perhaps accounting for 5 to 10 percent of the assembly work done in their families. Alice described her children's participation: "The kids hate it. They just really hate the job, but, um, they help out when I'm running behind, or when they have extra time off, or when they're home. Uh, there are maybe three weeks that go by, and they never touch it, and then there may be times go by, ya know, this weekend, I think. My daughter helped me for, let's see, two hours on Thursday night finishing up last week's kit. I think it took her two hours. She had ta do two boxes, and it took her that long, and then she helped me yesterday for an hour and a half." Another worker, who was well known for completing her work in record time, explained how she managed: "All the children work, um, at certain times of the year. Right now, the two oldest ones don't. They're not here enough to, to help do it. Because they have practice after school, and they don't get home till late. But the two youngest ones and my husband and I have been doing them. But when the kids aren't busy, they all help." Another arrangement involved assistance from retired parents or other older family members. Participating in the homework on a minimal but regular basis afforded the chance to visit and simultaneously be useful. Older people working for relatives accomplished about 10 percent of the assembly work. Three Riverton homeworkers who were related to each other received help regularly from an older relative: "My aunt comes over like one day a week and helps. She probably puts in like six hours a week. She helps me and Rita and Lil, so she like puts in one day a week with each of us…. On the day of my nephew's birthday, my aunt, my brother-in-law, and my sister and me sat there, and they put 'em together, and I got two presses, and they put 'em together as fast as they could, and me and my aunt were hittin' 'em, and I think we did three boxes in an hour. That was really good."

Sometimes, if a relative or family member was not available to help, the main contractor in the household would further subcontract the work to a friend or neighbor. Some of the workers had actually started out as subcontractors, and when an opening became available, they had the advantage of experience and were able to get their own contracts. In some cases, the person helping the contractor did not want to invest the time or energy in completing an entire kit each week and was satisfied to subcontract on a part-time basis. One farm operator in Prairie Hills, helped seasonally by a neighbor, reported, "Uh, the neighbor lady has been doing some of them for me, like through the busy times, spring and harvest. So, those times, why, I put in, I've been doing two-thirds of them. And I probably put in oh, twenty-five to thirty hours, and she probably puts in another ten or fifteen. And that's kinda the way it works." Gradually, that situation changed because the "neighbor lady" wanted more than seasonal income. The farm operator explained, "Lately, she's been doing 'em, helping me every week. She kinda wanted a little guaranteed money. So this winter she's been doing a third of them every week. And, we'll probably keep that arrangement right on through the summer." Robin, who has a part-time clerical job and glues grommets for TMC, began to subcontract her work out to a friend: "I have had her come in here three Sunday nights in a row and help me, or Sunday afternoons, I guess, we worked until about seven. And I did it strictly because for awhile I was feeling just really drained, like I wasn't gonna be able ta ever finish 'em."

In spite of many homeworkers describing their assembly work as shared, further probing revealed that, in most households, one adult was largely completing the kit. In Riverton, all but one of the contractors were women or women assembling with some help from their husbands. The home contractors of Prairie Hills were mostly women, but there was more male involvement in the work, partly because the boxes were too heavy for most women to lift. The pieces to assemble were not as small as those in Riverton, either. A few men explicitly called the homework in Riverton "women's work."

Homework as "women's work" added to the other tasks thought to be women's responsibilities. The major difficulty expressed by women contractors was how to keep up with housework and children while completing the kit. The women on farms often described how they fit farmwork into this schedule; they were aware that husbands and children rarely crossed over into housework. As Irene put it, "I do my parts and he comes home, and he cleans up. We have supper. He sits in his easy chair and I do parts. It's my job and I do it." Lucy agreed: "It doesn't bother him to be in here all day long, down watching his screen and his computer stuff, and having me out there and doing bolts."

Although more work in the home did not always mean all of the work was shared, most contractors believed that at least the potential for redistributing the work was there. Van and Myra operate a large hog farm. We chatted in their work space shed. Although Van admitted that he didn't help with housework, he put the homework in a different perspective: "I think I'm helping her. Now see, she was gonna have a job in town, which would have been eight hours a day, five days a week. It would have been forty hours. I couldn't have helped her in there. I can here [with the bolts]. Now I'm not maybe necessarily doing more help in the house than I ever did before or anything like that, but I do help do this, so I'm still helping her." Van's position was fairly typical of most homeworkers' husbands. They may not help with the housework, but when needed, they will pitch in with the assembly work.

The incorporation of waged work in the home varies according to the needs and abilities of the workers in the household. The potential to redistribute paid and unpaid work activities in the home exists, but the experiences of the homeworkers show that such redistribution usually occurs in accordance with the current division of labor by sex in the household. Locating the work in or around the home already contributed a great deal to defining homework as women's work. Treating homework, like housework and child care, as women's work underscores that women are responsible for the work, and male household members become "helpers" in the process. In this context, market relations are shaped by social relationships, which include and are embedded in gendered notions of the division of labor in the household and the local market.

Flexibility

From the perspective of TMC, the organization of home-based production is flexible, allowing TMC to vary the type and quantity of inventory as needed at no extra cost. The workers often cited flexibility as the main advantage of homeworking. For them, flexibility covers a broad range of aspects, such as autonomy in setting hours, ability to share the work within and between households, and the potential to accomplish other tasks along with the work. The assembly work has a pervasive touch once it enters the household. Time and space, the nature of work, and people are all made flexible by the interaction of paid and unpaid labor in the home.

Workers often discussed flexibility as the autonomy to set their own hours. The assembly work must be completed within a week, but within that week, the worker sets the schedule in accordance with other tasks and chores. Even the weekly deadline was somewhat flexible, as workers often spoke about the local managers "being real good" about reasonable extensions of time as long as the requests did not become regular. In terms of the flexibility of the schedule, there are several implications.

Norma, a Riverton homeworker, cited flexibility as a main advantage of the work, but described various aspects of it: "Well, it's up to us. I mean, that's the bottom line. You either work on it. We know the amount of screws we gotta get done. We know the amount of time it takes, and if we wanna bring it down to the wire, well, it's us that's gonna have to work our little butts off. I mean, if we were real, real smart, and put, you know, say five to six hours in every single day, you know, and got a real routine set up here, but then there's no flexibility. You know, that's no good, either." The reality that "the bolts have to be done" tends to govern one's schedule and activities. Other activities become a trade-off in terms of the time needed to complete a kit. Mollie is a young woman with six young children who assembles bolts in Riverton. She expressed the time trade-off as follows: "Your kit has to be done. Sometimes I'll take a day off, and I'll do the sort of things around the house that I know won't get done unless I just plain say 'tomorrow I'll just hafta punch bolts all day long in order to make up for the day before that I just had ta take time to do other things.'" Most workers express the time flexibility as an advantage because they see it as a matter of their choice. They can choose to put off the assembly work and do something else, recognizing that later they will have to make up for it.

Another aspect of the flexibility of time is that there are no boundaries to the work schedule, which means that although the worker sets the hours, she may also find that there are no "off-duty" hours. Homework is always there for the worker, regardless of what other tasks or activities took time during the day. Peggy, a young homeworker in Riverton, has tried to explain to others that the assembly work is time consuming when combined with other work, though it may not appear as such when the hours alone are considered: "It just takes time. That's what I tell most people. I said, 'Anybody can do it. It's just whether you wanna sit down and work five hours a day or not.' I think most people that I've heard think that you just go home and make a few parts a day, and you're gettin' paid, ya know. They don't realize that you gotta sit down for five hours or so, I would say a good five hours every day. I think a lotta mothers don't realize that that's a long time, in a way, when you still hafta get breakfast, dinner, and supper and do your laundry and lay 'em down for naps and things. I don't think they realize it's gonna take that much time."

The flexibility of one's homework schedule becomes dependent upon many aspects of the household: how much one can set working hours apart from family needs and desires, how to accomplish the work while attending to children and other chores and tasks, and the extent to which the worker is successful in getting other family members to contribute to the assembly work or the housework. Rita, a Riverton homeworker, discussed the difficulty of not having her work hours recognized within her family setting:

My husband thinks I should get the bolts done somehow, but yet I don't know when he thinks I'm supposed to do it. I haven't figured that out yet, because, no, he doesn't treat it…if I'm here, everything else is s'posed to be done, too, 'cause I'm home and at night, ya know, if I'm sitting there and the kids want somethin', he thinks I should be with the kids. He doesn't really treat it [as a job]…. I kinda wish I could set hours, I'm gonna work from this hour to this hour, and that's the way it's gonna be. I'm not gettin' up. This is my work time, ya know. But none of 'em can understand that if you try to set hours, they can't, ya know. They'll call you away for somethin' and, I have done it before. I said, "I'm not leaving. This is my job. I'm staying here. I'm working at this and that's all there is to it." I have done that to 'em before, and I'll sit there in the evening and I won't leave. I just work, and none of them like it. They don't like it when I stay back there and work, and they don't like it when I don't help them out, but once in a while, you just hafta do that once in a while so they can see it's a real job. Because I don't know otherwise how, some weeks it is hard to get it done. The week goes and you've done this and that and all, you don't get it done.

Informal labor done in the home means the worker is responsible for setting boundaries that are ordinarily set by the outside workplace and that allow one to accomplish one's work relatively uninterrupted by family needs and concerns. Whereas the formal workplace concretely separates home and work for the worker, the homeworker is responsible for maintaining that separation while working in the home. This flexibility leaves Rita more capable of responding to family needs when necessary, such as picking up a sick child from school, but also results in greater conflict and tension over how to set aside adequate working time in order to accomplish the work. Rita also expresses the difficulty of accomplishing work that is not taken seriously as work. Because of its flexible organization of production, because it is done in the home at odd hours of the day and night by Rita and whomever else may be available and willing to help, homework lacks the form and status of a "real job" in the view of those around her.

This lack of formal boundaries between unpaid and paid work allows work to infiltrate many areas of the home. Many women homeworkers stated that "being home for my children while I earn money" is an important advantage of the assembly work. Most of these homeworkers also believed that working in the home affected their time and ability to care for their children and that their children's needs and presence often determined their time and ability to work. One man who assembled bolts at home during a period of unemployment commented that one improvement would be to get "a babysitter once in a while so you could do a little more work." Some of the homeworkers reported using this alternative occasionally, but it was seen as defeating one purpose of working at home, which was precisely to save on the costs of child care as well as to be present for one's children while working. Two ex-homeworkers commented on the challenge of working on bolts while taking care of young children. One explained, "Um, the bit about, as far as a mother staying home with the kids, so she can be with her kids. That's not gonna work. 'Cause she actually can't be with her kids when she's doing this. There's no way. I mean, kids have to be in bed at night so she can work and still do it.... Well, that's the way it was really broadcast. You know, you can stay home with the kids, you can stay home with the kids. And like I told you, that's not true. Because you can't do it with your kids. They have to be in bed. They cannot be standing there and you're entertaining 'em.... That's what they [TMC] want to make it. And it's not. There's no way. They're trying to make it family." The other advised, "I wouldn't recommend it for a mother with young kids, not unless she was really strict.... Because I don't think you can pay attention to your kids and do this job if, ya know, in the back of your head you thought, I'm gonna be home with my kids, and I'm gonna be the perfect mother and all this stuff, because your kids are more deprived than if you went outside and someone was watching the kids."

The experience of most homeworkers with young children was that the assembly work and child care could both be performed, although usually not at the same time. Most of these homeworkers clearly viewed their children and family as their first priority, putting the work second at best. Yet as the weekly deadline approached, the bolts would assume a higher priority, pushing other needs temporarily to the side. Flexibility comes to mean that the worker juggles family needs with work requirements; how the different needs are juggled changes from day to day. Children, housework, and assembly homework form a continuous cycle to which women homeworkers respond throughout each day and evening.

Homework provides the flexibility for women to engage in wage labor while remaining in the home. Proponents of homework often assert that home-based work can resolve women's conflicts between outside wage labor and attending to family needs. Yet the conflict seems to remain unresolved for many of the women homeworkers. Bringing the work into the home adds to their work, extending the work day. The other needs and tasks do not disappear and usually are not considered by the family or the worker to be as flexible as the homework.

Families often assume that their lives will continue as usual. Women homeworkers find themselves dealing with the same situation as women who work outside the home: the double day, or double sets of expectations about work.

Women become flexible in this context: Women's time becomes flexible to accommodate the work. A woman's work space becomes flexible as her family requests that she work beyond their vision and hearing. Flexibility goes well beyond the autonomy to set hours; indeed, it is somewhat questionable to what extent this autonomy exists. In many of these households, women homeworkers become flexible according to the multiple demands of family, home, and work.

The division of labor in most of the households studied followed a pattern in which men were largely responsible for wage labor or/and farm operation. In only one household was the man described as actively in charge of cooking, cleaning, and child rearing in addition to his outside job; his wife, however, is the homeworker. This family was not a farming household. In none of the active farm households were males described as equal participants in domestic tasks. In contrast, the women in the farming households often crossed over into farmwork while still retaining responsibility for major household work and the assembly homework. These general patterns varied little by the ages of the women and men interviewed.

Between women and men homeworkers, flexibility varied in quantity as well as quality. Across the two communities, there were eight men who were the main homeworkers in their households. These men were more likely than the women homeworkers to subcontract part of the work out to other people or to hire labor to help with the farmwork, but they did not take on greater domestic or family responsibilities. They dealt with flexible production by hiring help and maintaining the separation between work and home. Women experienced the flexibility of homework as an activity that absorbed all spaces of free time in between other major responsibilities of child care, housework, farmwork, and outside wage labor. Women's flexibility centers on their ability to cross over into all spheres of labor, while men's roles are defined in such a way that men can avoid entering the sphere of "women's work." In many households, the assembly work was defined as women's work, leaving women solely responsible for it.

Housework, child rearing, and sometimes assembly homework are not casually defined as "women's work." The definition of what is strictly women's sphere of activity enters the realm of strongly held values and beliefs ordering family life and influencing activities both inside and outside the home. These beliefs are so deeply accepted by women and men that it was commonplace for a woman with only male children to assume that there was no one to help out with the household chores. Or, as one ex-homeworker explained, "I have my 'hired' girls: the washing machine, dryer, and dishwasher are working with me all day long." It was also common for women to speak of household tasks and child rearing in the possessive form: my cleaning, my cooking and baking, being home with my children. Men, too, used language to define the boundaries of these activities: "She doesn't deep clean the way she used to," or "Sometimes I help her with the dishes or the kids." Tanya, a young home-worker with three children, defined *housewife* as "married to the house" and responsible for all the chores. When such chores combined with child rearing and assembly work, conflict sometimes resulted from her sense of overload: "If I have a bad day where I don't get enough bolts and stuff done, I wish he would pitch in more. If he would help with the laundry or whatever, the dishes, make a meal. But we just fight about it and then I have to do it anyways. I might just as well do it." Although women mentioned housework as a distraction from the tedium of the bolts, men did not. Janice and Ken share the assembly work but definitely do not share the housework: "Last night he was gettin' really tired of doin' bolts, and I said, 'Well, I'll do the bolts, and you do the dishes.' He said, 'I'll do the bolts, and you do the dishes.' Ya know, he don't do dishes, and so I don't think anything really changes. He would rather do them [bolts] than anything else, and there are times I won't do them 'cause I know I've got these other things to do, and it's just impossible [to do both]."

The theme of flexibility is illustrative of ways in which the household con-text shapes the process of production in informal sector work. The household incorporates homework into the existing division of labor, adding waged labor to unpaid housework and child care so that it becomes an extension of house-hold activities. Differences between women and men homeworkers show how the same work embedded in household contexts can be organized differently and incorporated into different clusters of work activities because of the gen-dered division of labor.

Conclusion

Industrial homeworking in these communities illuminates the importance of understanding market exchange relations in the context of local community and household relations. The creation of homeworking jobs in these commu-nities resulted from the states' willingness to support and subsidize the restruc-turing and relocation of production from Detroit to rural areas. In addition to financing, developers and leaders in the local communities helped shape the newly created jobs as women's work. The local business elite supported home-working by recruiting workers: men for the warehouse jobs and women for the home contractor positions. Along with state development officers, local offi-cials were active in promoting the notions of supplemental income and sec-ondary work and in applying those concepts to women's work; in doing so, they regulated and contributed to the development of the work and to the con-struction of the gendered nature of the work.

Household dynamics, including the sexual division of labor, also contributed to the regulation of homeworking and to the assignment of such work to women. The organization and process of production evolve in the context of the household, shaping the labor as it is incorporated into other paid and unpaid work activities. Thus, there was variation from one household to another on such issues as participation, development of work spaces, and ways of accomplishing the work. However, the consistency of the gendered division of labor in the household strongly shaped homeworking in such a way that most households regarded the work as "women's work." Although there is some room for individual and household variation in the work, the acceptance of such a division of labor frequently meant that the worker incorporated homework into his or her primary sphere of activity. Women workers often observed that homework was an extension of their unpaid labor in the home; men homeworkers saw the work more as an extension of their paid work activities. These men experienced much less difficulty in separating the work from family and household needs; in fact, they rarely mentioned work boundaries as a problem, probably because they were more likely to work on their property but outside the home. Men were also more likely to subcontract the work out, setting up a quasi-employer relationship with neighbors or friends.

The interactive context of paid and unpaid work in the home gave a new meaning to the concept of flexibility for women homeworkers. The structure of the work was somewhat flexible, but most women workers found themselves becoming more flexible in response to the multiple demands of home, work, and family needs. As one homeworker put it, "I can go out to work and come home and still have everything to do here on top of that. Or I can work at home, and do my housework along the way." Implicit in her statement is that in either work situation, she still carries the responsibility for the unpaid work in the home; she can choose when rather than whether to fit it in. As one homeworker's husband observed, "She's worth more at home, especially now when she can bring in an extra income from the home." As a homeworker, she becomes indispensable in maintaining the household: She accomplishes housework and child care, which would be costs if she worked outside the home, and she earns money by homeworking in and around those other tasks.

Homeworkers are "worth more" in other ways, too. The wages they earn do not challenge the local wage structure, and, at the same time, portions of those wages are cycled through the local economy. When workers stop homeworking, they are not counted among the unemployed, nor are they able to draw unemployment benefits. Women as homeworkers do not challenge the division of labor in the local job market; rather, homeworking reinforces both the low wage structure and local occupational segregation. The states, in supporting homeworking as development, are financing the maintenance of local class and gender relations. With production reorganized and relocated, the social relations that form its context merely become more entrenched.

Notes

1   The research on which this essay is based was supported by a Rural Policy Fellowship from the Woodrow Wilson Foundation, 1988–1990. This chapter is based on the author's larger study, titled *Getting By: Women Homeworkers and Rural Economic Development*, (Lawrence: University Press of Kansas, 1994). Used with permission of the publisher.

2   The names of cities, local firms, and people have been changed to maintain confidentiality.

3   Osha Gray Davidson, *Broken Heartland: The Rise of America's Rural Ghetto* (New York and Toronto: The Free Press, 1990); and Mark Friedberger, *Farm Families and Change in Twentieth Century America* (Lexington: The University Press of Kentucky, 1988).

4   Gringeri, *Getting By.*

5   Enzo Mingione, *Fragmented Societies: A Sociology of Economic Life Beyond the Market Paradigm* (Cambridge, Mass.: Basil Blackwell, 1991).

6   I tape-recorded and transcribed all interviews, which were analyzed for themes such as the the process of development, the process and organization of production, working conditions, flexibility, and the meaning of ideas such as supplemental income and part-time work. Field notes based on participant observation of homeworkers and field research experiences added to the interview data and were used to confirm patterns.

7   TMC managers told me they developed this idea based on observations of rural homeworking in Japan during a 1982 trip. Apparently, rural residents in Japan were assembling large automotive parts, such as dashboards, at home or in their barns.

8   Two residents from the northern community told me that when TMC proposed the homeworking jobs to the planning commission, the local developers were open to the idea but felt that TMC could offer better wages to the workers. Such a response may have led TMC managers to conclude that the demand for work there would not meet their requirements.

9   There's a certain irony to this statement about unemployment. Indeed, there are fewer unemployment benefits paid because TMC defines the workers as independent contractors and therefore does not pay unemployment taxes. Fewer people from this pool of workers will receive unemployment benefits than if they held outside jobs because their classification as independent contractors renders them ineligible for payment when there is no assembly work available.

10   Kathleen Christensen, "Home-Based Clerical Work: No Simple Truth, No Single Reality," in *Homework: Historical and Contemporary Perspectives on Paid Labor*

at Home, eds. Eileen Boris and Cynthia R. Daniels (Urbana and Chicago: University of Illinois Press, 1989), pp. 183–197.

11 Eleven of the thirty-six households in Riverton, or about one-third, were farming households. The remainder were rural nonfarm households. In Prairie Hills, thirty-two of the forty-eight households were farm operations; the remainder were rural nonfarm households.

12 A kit is a week's worth of pieces to be assembled by the homeworker. In Prairie Hills, homeworkers assembled 5,400 suspension bolts per week and were paid anywhere from 2.5 to 3.8 cents per finished bolt. Each bolt had eight to eleven components to assemble. In Riverton, homeworkers were pressing small screws and bolts together; with the very small screws there were about 21,000 pieces to assemble each week. Larger screw assemblies had 11,000 to 18,000 pieces to assemble per week. These kits in Riverton paid $0.00857 to $0.012 per screw assembly. Overall, wages per hour averaged lower in Riverton ($3.00) than in Prairie Hills ($4.50). Average hours worked per week were higher in Riverton (45 to 50 hours) than in Prairie Hills (35 to 40 hours).

13 The JTPA was federal legislation that distributed funds in part to train workers who had been displaced by industrial restructuring, relocation, or economic changes, such as farmers displaced by the agricultural recession of the 1980s.

14 Davidson, *Broken Heartland*, and Janet Fitchen, *Endangered Spaces, Enduring Places: Change, Identity, and Survival in Rural America* (Boulder, Colo.: Westview Press, 1991).

11

Biases in Labor Law

A Critique from the Standpoint of Home-Based Workers

« *Elisabeth Prügl*

ON SEPTEMBER 15, 1976, LILIAN DOROTHY GOOKEY APPEARED BEFORE THE Industrial Tribunal in London North. The proceedings were to decide whether her work giver was required to provide her with what amounted to an employment contract. Her work giver, Mr. Standing, owner of Expert Clothing Services & Sales Ltd., denied that Gookey was an employee of his company, arguing instead that she was self-employed. Gookey had started to work for Expert Clothing Services & Sales Ltd. in 1946 making trousers and slacks. At that time, there were about thirty employees in the company, all of whom Standing admitted had employee status. Gookey was paid by the piece, including a bonus per hour, and worked a basic forty hours per week.

Over the years, Standing gradually reduced his work force. In 1969, he closed the operation, but Gookey continued to work for him in her home. In 1976, Standing wanted to decrease Gookey's working hours from the regular forty to twenty-two and cut her pay accordingly. He argued that he could do so because she was now self-employed. The Industrial Tribunal in London North ruled against him, deciding that Gookey had been an employee since 1946 who was entitled to annual leave, sick leave, and remuneration as fixed by the Wages Council for her trade and whose hours of work should be forty per week.[1]

Balamma Goraya is a home-based bidi worker in Ahmedabad, India.[2] She has been rolling bidis for Jivraj Seth, one of the leading manufacturers in town, for twenty-eight years. Until recently she was treated by Seth as an employee. Her work routine involved visiting Seth's shop every Saturday to turn in the bidis she had rolled during the week; get paid for her labor; and pick up a new batch of leaves, string, and tobacco. Suddenly one day, Seth changed the rules. He no longer gave out raw materials to the bidi homeworkers but required that they buy raw materials from him. In turn, he bought back the finished bidis. Balamma Goraya's contract of employment was turned into a commercial relationship. She no longer sold her labor but was considered a self-employed worker who marketed her products. Her work did not change, but she lost all rights guaranteed under the Indian Bidi and Cigar Workers (Conditions of Employment) Act.[3]

Experiences like those of Lilian Gookey and Balamma Goraya are legion in countries throughout the world.[4] To a large degree they derive from a desire of employers to cut costs by evading labor laws. Treating Gookey as self-employed would have allowed Standing more flexibility, he would have saved considerable costs associated with mandated benefits as well as with employee protection from dismissal. By turning Goraya into a self-employed person, Seth is no longer under obligation to pay her minimum wages or to grant her annual leave with wages or maternity leave. He can now dismiss her at will and can resume the practice of randomly rejecting as substandard bidis that she rolled.

The negative impact of self-employment status for home-based workers is clear. As a single woman who had worked for the same employer for years, Gookey was concerned about her pension. Had she accepted being designated as self-employed, Standing would not have had any obligation to continue stamping her pension card. She also would have lost considerable income and would not have qualified for redundancy payments when she was laid off. For Goraya, being treated as self-employed meant lower pay, more drudgery, and exposure to Seth's whims.

Although it seems intuitively clear that it is unjust to treat underpaid and overworked home-based workers as self-employed, there is considerable confusion over their employment status. Agents of states around the world deal with homeworkers in a contradictory manner. In India, for example, the researcher who described Balamma Goraya's experience found that labor inspectors did not know that the Bidi and Cigar Workers (Conditions of Employment) Act covered homeworkers, although the Indian Supreme Court had ruled that it did. The chief labor inspector in Gujarat asked, "How [could] somebody working in a private house...ever be an employee?"[5]

In Britain most courts have determined that homeworkers are employees. Yet, Inland Revenue officials have taken the opposite position, arguing that homeworkers are not employees because they "are not bound by the conditions of normal employment. They work for any number of principals, or they work when they like, and for such hours as they want. No notice is legally required from either party of termination [of contract]."[6] Similarly, in the United States different government agencies use different definitions of *employee*. Although the Labor Department relies on interpretations of the Fair Labor Standards Act (FLSA), which tend to classify homeworkers as employees, the Internal Revenue Service (IRS) applies common law criteria, which do not yield a precise categorization of homeworkers. Furthermore, if the IRS finds that an employer has wrongly treated a worker as self-employed, Section 530 of the tax code permits the employer to continue such treatment while allowing the worker to pay taxes as an employee.[7]

Homeworkers are themselves often unsure about their employment status or do not know their rights. In India, researchers for the Self Employed Women's Association (SEWA) found that bidi homeworkers in towns that were not unionized did not know that they were eligible to receive minimum wages and other benefits under the law.[8] Professional and clerical homeworkers in Silicon Valley, California, are equally ignorant. They call themselves "free-lancers" or "independent contractors" but do not know whether they are self-employed or employees.[9]

The International Labour Organisation (ILO) is discussing whether it should establish an international standard to improve the working conditions of home-based workers and define their employment status. Only three previous ILO conventions mention homeworkers at all. The Minimum Wage Fixing Machinery Convention of 1928 commits governments to set up such a machinery in areas where no mechanism exists to fix wages through collective bargaining, "in particular in home working trades." The Convention Concerning Sickness Insurance of 1928 stipulates that there should be compulsory sickness insurance for "manual and non-manual workers, including apprentices, ... out-workers and domestic servants." And the revised Maternity Protection Convention of 1952 applies to "women in industrial undertakings and in non-industrial and agricultural occupations, including women wage earners working at home."[10] In these conventions, governments deemed it necessary to refer to homeworkers specifically. It is not clear whether they would have been included otherwise. In other words, it is not clear whether the category of worker, as used by the ILO, includes homeworkers and whether they are covered in ILO conventions if they are not mentioned.

The majority of homeworkers around the world are women.[11] There is a widespread understanding that they are housewives who want to earn some pin money and whose work is merely a hobby. The corollary to the woman in this perception is the husband-breadwinner on whose income the women depend. Labor law is formulated around the notion of the male worker who is defined as a breadwinner, and housewife status seems to preclude status as workers.

This chapter shows that labor law institutionalizes an understanding of employees that tends to preclude home-based workers from its ambit. I also show that the confusion about the employment status of homeworkers does not derive only from employers' self-interest and from public perceptions. Masculinist biases that permeate the law itself produce homeworkers' insecure status. Criteria used to test employee status often describe the situations of factory and office workers. The control test—the most widely accepted test of employee status—denies homeworkers employee status precisely because they do not work in a public place where they can be continuously supervised. Other tests of employment status do not work for homeworkers because they are dualistically conceived, opposing employers to employees and failing to consider the hybrid status of workers who combine characteristics of employees and the self-employed. By taking the employer-employee opposition as constitutive, labor law discourse denies the diversity of the work experiences of "atypical" female workers.

Gender Bias in the Control Test

In most countries around the world, homeworkers do not have a separate legal status and therefore have to fit the category of employee in order to qualify for protection under labor laws. Of 144 states surveyed by the ILO in the late 1980s, only twenty made an effort in their laws to define homeworkers in a way that takes into account the specific characteristics of their work organization and their relationships to their work givers.[12] An additional five mentioned homeworkers but did not define them, and sixteen more required that homeworkers prove they are employees in order to benefit from the provisions of the law. The rest, 103 countries, did not mention homeworkers in their labor laws at all. By default, homeworkers in these countries did not qualify for protection unless they fit the category of employee. That is, in 124 countries (86 percent of all cases), homeworkers had to prove that they were employees before they could expect to receive any protection under labor laws.

In general, labor law distinguishes between employees and the self-employed by looking at the type of contracts that exist between workers and their work givers. A "contract of service" implies that the relationship between the contracting parties is one of employer and employee. In contrast, a "contract for services" denotes a temporally limited engagement that is regarded as a commercial exchange; this type of contract legally identifies a worker as self-employed. However, different countries use different indicators in order to determine whether a contract is "of service" or "for services." Indeed, an ILO effort to establish internationally valid principles had to be abandoned because of the complexity of the issue.[13]

Yet, there are some principles for identifying employee status that have gained wide currency through the diffusion of continental and common law traditions.[14] One principle that legislators, lawyers, and judges in both traditions have applied to determine whether a worker is an employee is the principle of subordination. An employment contract is said to exist if a worker is subordinate to the provider of work. A variety of criteria are applied to determine whether subordination exists, some unique to common law, others shared by the continental law tradition.

The most common indicator of subordination, which is employed in both continental and common law, is whether a worker is under the control of an employer.[15] For homeworkers this control test is extremely problematic. According to some legal arguments, middlemen, merchants, and employers do not have control over homeworkers because they cannot supervise workers who do not work on their premises and because they do not have "disciplinary power" over them. Middlemen, merchants, jobbers, and factory owners cannot prescribe hours of work for homeworkers or discipline homeworkers if they do not organize their tasks in the prescribed way. Furthermore, they do not instruct homeworkers as to the place where they must carry out their work. Indeed, in the United States, common law criteria used to indicate employee status include whether a worker follows set hours of work, works full-time for an employer, and does the work on the employer's premises.[16] These criteria immediately disqualify homeworkers who set their own work hours and work intermittently in their homes. Under the control test neither Lilian Gookey nor Balamma Goraya would qualify as employees.[17]

The lack of attention labor law has given to home-based workers and the counter-intuitive results of the control test cannot be understood unless we recall the fact that most homeworkers are women. Feminist research has documented that understandings of who is a worker involve presumptions about gender. State policies have contributed to constructing workers as husbands and breadwinners, i.e., men who support their wives and children. Until recently, unions demanded and employers often paid a "family wage" that maintained a presumed male worker together with his dependents. The control test similarly implies a stereotypical image of the male worker, one who typically works outside the private home. It thus fails to account for the lived realities of homeworkers.[18]

the HWA has targeted the bottom. The campaign on both the public and political level against the targeted large companies has been challenging and often exciting, but the actual organizing of the homeworkers themselves has proved to be the most daunting and also the most stimulating task.

The ILGWU could not organize homeworkers alone. The union had to work within the (targeted) Chinese community and make links to key people and begin developing a profile in the Chinese press and in the Vietnamese community. Organizing in nontraditional areas where unions had little or no stronghold, or where the women had little or no experience with a trade union (and if they had, it was more than likely a negative one), meant that the union had to commit to an extremely long-term and patient approach. The campaign had to focus around years of work rather than just months. Trade unions could learn from some examples of grassroots women's organizing outside of trade unions; I refer particularly to SEWA in India. However, trade unions have historically been reluctant to engage in this form of organizing. Part of the reason is the inordinate amount of time and resources needed. Meanwhile, there are generally plenty of nonunion plants and offices to organize where workers are conveniently clustered in large numbers.

To escape the "blame the victim" approach, long common among traditional trade unionists, HWA looks at the reasons that women end up doing homework in the first place. Once one understands these reasons, it is possible to develop an organizing strategy to adapt to the situation. In the future, organizing cannot just mean simply passing out leaflets at plant or office gates because these plants and offices are rapidly disappearing into people's homes.

The preunion, or associate, local is an excellent way to gradually introduce workers to the concept of unionism. It can be a less intimidating option or a first step for someone who may never have been a union member or has no knowledge of what a union is. A functioning local can determine its own bylaws and elect its own executive. It can provide services, legal advocacy, lobbying, and other political work. HWA is thought to be the first associate membership local in the country. Members pay an annual membership fee of CDN$12.

Programs, services, and events are organized by the union office, which means that members of the Association routinely come to the office for meetings and use it as a pick-up point for outings and trips. The office functions not simply as an administrative office of the union but also as a drop-in center for members of the community. Toys and materials have been collected for children and are set up in "the children's room," formerly the room of a business agent. HWA staff offer counseling and referral to other community organizations for a variety of legal problems. Through networking among organizations serving the Chinese community, homeworkers are also referred back to HWA.

The biggest challenges in organizing homeworkers are locating them and understanding the underground network of contracting and homeworking. Since homeworkers are not clustered in one plant, the focus must be on locating individual homes because this is their place of employment. A researcher might simply hang around traditional garment areas and follow cars that pick up bundles of cut goods from contracting shops. This method, however, is extremely labor intensive and time consuming. It is more effective to establish an underground word-of-mouth system and develop a profile and a reputation in the community. Advertising in ethnic newspapers and local radio and television stations brought HWA and its phone number before people. A hotline service for homeworkers, with a separate telephone line from the main union line, was particularly effective at the beginning of the organizing campaign. Advertising the hotline service for homeworker rights in the same sections of the newspapers that routinely advertise for homeworkers also paid off.

Word-of-mouth organizing is crucial for gaining support and recognition within the community. If the association is able to achieve something for one homeworker, then often that same homeworker will speak about it with her friends. The network is informal and fluctuating but is there and must be tapped. Many of the new members have come because of referrals from other members.

Throughout 1992, HWA offered monthly legal clinics and social teas on Saturday afternoons. A volunteer lawyer came for a Saturday afternoon to meet with homeworkers on a drop-in basis, and a social tea afterward provided an opportunity for homeworkers to get together informally. This program helped break up the isolation of being a homeworker. HWA provided day care for all events because without it many of the women could not participate. One of the most successful organizing methods was the promotion of trips on Saturdays in the warmer months. The first summer, HWA organized a weekly trip to a variety of places of interest, chartering a bus and setting up a program. Members received reduced-price tickets as an incentive to join, and the trips included their families.

After one year of action, membership renewals were required. Renewals became the litmus test for the success of the servicing and organizing concept behind HWA because without a long-term commitment from the members, HWA could not survive. Renewals were encouraging, and there was an increase in new membership. But the HWA coordinator has found that turnovers will become a problem because homeworkers often experience cycles of employment in factories. HWA will have to develop a system to maintain contact with members as well to adapt to their fluctuating work situations.

Programs offered by HWA must meet members' needs. In September 1992, HWA established an English as a second language (ESL) class for three hours on Sunday afternoons, with day care. The Toronto Board of Education provided instruction. This very successful program has served as a recruitment station for new members. Homeworkers agreed on the timing and design of the program. Participation has risen from an initial ten homeworkers to more than twenty, and there is a waiting list.[17]

All HWA members now receive a Chinese newsletter. A benefit plan was introduced for homeworkers in early 1993 that includes a prescription-drug and sickness plan. As a result of its many decades of running benefit and pension funds for factory workers, the union has much experience in this area. One benefit plan had been sitting idle, and revision of the legal trust agreement for that plan and support from the union trustees of the fund meant that a plan could be developed for homeworkers. Unlike other funds that run from employer contributions, the ILGWU could charge a membership fee for the benefit plan far below the cost of other individual plans as a result of the investment income from the fund and a surplus from employers who had paid into the plan in the past. HWA has attracted some new members as a result of the introduction of this plan, but not as many as expected. Because there is an up-front membership cost, there might be initial reluctance. It is hoped that as HWA members experience the plan, it may become more attractive to "unorganized" homeworkers.

HWA conducted a pilot women's leadership training course for homeworkers in the winter of 1994. The aim of the program was to provide training for homeworkers on a wide variety of issues such as piece rates, politics, labor law, the restructuring in the garment industry, women's health and family or marital relations. The course emerged out of a very successful and well-attended information session on marital relations, and this session has even been repeated because of numerous requests. A very successful seminar on piecework extended the work of HWA in assisting homeworkers to further develop their skills in bargaining with contractors.

The leadership training program, building on a year of seminars and information sessions, had a core group of HWA members who attended weekly participatory workshops for eight consecutive Sunday afternoons. The course provided an opportunity to develop the indigenous leadership of the HWA. As one homeworker said at the end of the course, "I must now talk to other homeworkers about their rights as a butterfly travels from flower to flower." The leadership course enabled homeworkers to take a more active role in setting the priorities for action by the Coalition and designing the main agenda of activities for HWA in the next year.

As with most organizing, there is no one magic wand or technique that will work to organize homeworkers. A variety of creative techniques must be developed, tried, and retried. For instance, for the first social tea, only one homeworker showed up. As trust in the staff members of the HWA grew, so did participation in the various events. Now participants in the social teas have to be politely told when it is time to go home!

Our goal is to eventually be in a position where it will be possible to organize some of the HWA members into a full-fledged union with a formal collective bargaining relationship. However, legal barriers remain in Ontario for homeworkers to exercise freedom of choice to join a trade union and bargain collectively.[18] The Ontario Labor Relations Board has not recognized homeworkers as employees. Earlier labor board decisions had taken homeworkers out of bargaining units. We will have to win an argument in front of the Labor Board that homeworkers are employees. This will be difficult because most homeworkers deviate from traditional definitions of who are employees; most homeworkers are multiple job-holders and own their own machinery. Our goal will be to make a case for a new definition of employee that would embrace homeworkers.

In addition, the Chinese community generally has had little or no experience with trade unions and exhibits a strong distrust of central organizations. With time and patience, we believe that we can build a culture of homework unionism in these Chinese workers' adopted country. A fundamental problem remains: This kind of organizing takes a lot of resources. It is crucial to have a staff member who develops programs and is available to provide assistance to the members. Once the membership grows, it becomes increasingly difficult for this staff member to organize in new areas. The ILGWU and HWA will be attempting to raise funds so that there can be a full-time homeworker organizer as well as a staff member for services only. The HWA is very service oriented, which obviously requires a much higher staff-to-membership ratio than what is considered normal in traditional union circles. The concept of a union steward in a plant who can handle a lot of the union servicing does not fit in this case. Expensive staffing cannot be funded solely by the dues revenue from the association—the membership dues have to be low, because of members' low incomes. The long-term success of this form of organizing will require a commitment from the union to subsidize HWA with main dues revenue. The difficulty for the ILGWU Ontario region is that the regular dues base is in serious decline as the plant closure rate continues to climb. As the need to put more resources into this organizing becomes greater, the ILGWU is increasingly unable to fund it from its regular dues base. Fortunately, HWA has received substantial government funding (in particular from the Ontario Women's Directorate), which has allowed it to develop its ideas and fund the staff required up to this point. This funding base, however, is precarious, and other sources of more stable funds will have to be raised in order to continue organizing over the long run. Other sources of government funding should enable HWA to develop a leadership training program and to continue providing services.

Experience has shown that in order to really be able to develop this kind of organizing over the long run, it is necessary to begin it before any crisis in membership occurs. The ILGWU had already experienced dramatic loss of membership, and there would have been fewer financial difficulties had this program begun a decade before it did. One of HWA's roles can be to maintain the program as long as possible, continuing to fundraise but also encouraging more stable unions to begin similar campaigns now, before significant membership loss renders them less effective and less able to develop aggressive new and costly campaigns.

A shortage of funds has also meant that HWA has been unable to expand much beyond the initial targeted community. Two Portuguese and two Filipino women recently joined HWA, becoming the first members who do not speak Cantonese or Vietnamese. Because the strength of HWA has been the high number of services in the members' native tongues, it would require staff with capability in other languages to really develop HWA in other communities. HWA has discussed the possibility of organizing volunteers in other languages, but concern remains that such services would be patchwork, dependent on the availability of the various volunteers. This issue will be a recurring one for HWA's consideration. Currently staff can speak Cantonese, Spanish, Italian, and Tamil. We have begun an outreach program to homeworkers in the Spanish and South-Asian communities, funded by the "Jobs Ontario Community Action" project for one year (1995). We intend to seek additional funding. The problem remains that such funding is only for one year projects which makes program existence precarious.

The reaction of union members in the factories to HWA has evolved. Initially there was a lot of resistance to investing staff time and union resources in homeworkers. But this reluctance has gradually been overcome, particularly among members of the District Council (the governing body of the local union). A special session in the summer of 1992 helped immensely in reducing competition between the two groups. Union activists from the factories met with active members of HWA at a weekend conference. That experience was crucial to begin the development of a cohesive union approach to the changing structure of the garment industry in Canada. We need more educational work on this issue. As plant closures continue to climb in the garment sector in Ontario, so do reactionary responses to these closures, which tend to blame homeworkers and others who must work for less.

There have been numerous discussions about the possibility of forming a central (national) union committee that could pool financial resources to actually mount this kind of organizing on a larger scale. It would be appropriate for the Canadian Labor Congress (CLC—the equivalent of the AFL-CIO central labor organization in the United States) to take on this project. There should be a well-defined system for bringing new members into full-fledged unions and sorting out which union they should go into. The CLC has been supportive of the HWA initiative, but as yet it has made no commitment to expand or be actively involved in developing new organizing approaches. There has also been general discussion about the need to form a working women's association (similar to the Women's Union in Holland) that could be the backbone of a preunion for many women who cannot easily form a traditional trade union. Such an association could be based on a model like HWA but in a broader form and not confined to one targeted sector.

The challenge for labor is large as capital becomes more global and as the nature of work changes. Labor unions must rethink their methods and structures, but I believe the challenge can be met. Unions in Canada have gradually moved away from business unionism to more social unionism, but there is a new imperative to shift again. Community unionism may be the answer to some of labor's problems. It expands on social unionism by advocating that unions become integrally involved within their communities and form coalitions. As the power of capital consolidates, it becomes even more important for unions to expand beyond their traditional base.[19] HWA and the ILGWU Ontario region will continue the work described in this chapter. Although the Ontario government has not yet introduced its promised legislation, and as we learn of the beginnings of a major concerted effort by two key Canadian retailers to oppose this legislation, we know that the struggle will not be easy. But it is also increasingly evident that if the labor movement in Canada is to just maintain the strength it now holds (37.4 percent of the Canadian work force is unionized),[20] it must learn to organize the precarious work force as the core work force continues to shrink. Unions cannot afford to fight with each other to organize these remaining units. Instead, they must learn how to reach out to the peripheral and vulnerable work force. Otherwise, the labor movement will lose its core and will also become a peripheral force in the Canadian economy.

Notes

As this collection was going to press, the ILGWU was merging with the Amalgamated Clothing and Textile Workers Union (ACTWU) to form The Union of Needletrades, Industrial and Textile Employees (UNITE).

1 This description came from Holly Du, coordinator of the Homeworkers' Association.

2 Unless otherwise specified, ILGWU will refer to the Ontario region.

3 Meeting with Jay Mazur, New York City, May 14, 1992.

4 Statistics Canada, Employment, Earnings and Hours 72–002 and City of Toronto Planning Dept. Employment Statistics, 1992.

5 Statistics Canada, "Size of Firms," cat. no. 72–002, 1991. The union view is that these figures are a low estimation of the real number of small contracting and subcontracting shops.

6 For other documentation of this trend, see Swasti Mitter, *Common Fate, Common Bond: Women in the Global Economy* (London: Pluto Press, 1986); and Annie Phizacklea, *Unpacking the Fashion Industry: Gender, Racism, and Class in Production* (London: Routledge, 1990).

7 Carla Lipsig-Mumme, "Women in the Clothing Trade," *Studies in Political Economy* 22 (1987): 41–71.

8 See Hudson Bay Company, *1991 Annual Reports*; and "Overview of the Canadian Apparel Sector," Canadian Apparel Federation 1991 Annual Meeting.

9 *Canadian Financial Post*, May 11, 1993.

10 This research was funded by the Ontario Technology Fund, Technology Adjustment Research Fund. Researchers were Dr. Barbara Cameron and Teresa Mak. This is a province of Ontario research program through which the ILGWU Ontario region as well as sixteen other unions were able to investigate the impact of technological change and work reorganization.

11 The garment industry has always followed the waves of immigration, often being their first or only source of employment. The ILGWU Ontario region estimates that roughly 50 to 60 percent of the workers in the garment industry are of South-East Asian background.

12 In 1993, the ILGWU Ontario region completed a second study. The HWA researcher interviewed forty-five women who had not been previously interviewed. The results mirrored the first study. Importantly, the second study found that, on average, women's wages as homeworkers were drastically lower than their factory wages. On average, as homeworkers, women made CDN$4.00 to $5.00 per hour less than in the factory.

13 Barbara Cameron and Teresa Mak, "Working Conditions of Chinese-Speaking Homeworkers in the Toronto Garment Industry: Summary of the Results of a Survey Conducted by the ILGWU," mimeo, n.d.

14 The purpose of this chapter is to outline the initial stages of the campaign to organize homeworkers. Throughout 1993 and 1994, the main work of the Coalition for homeworkers was to pressure for legislative changes to the Ontario Employment Standards Act (ESA) to aid homeworkers. The details of the legislative work are beyond the scope of the chapter. By the summer of 1994, legislative change was not forthcoming; however, the Coalition had won the battle for smaller regulatory changes. Specifically, regulations to the ESA were changed

so that (1) homeworkers would receive 10 percent above the minimum wage to help cover electricity, heat, and equipment purchases; (2) homeworkers were now eligible for overtime pay; (3) homeworkers were entitled to a written contract of wages and working conditions.

15 We targeted Alfred Sung for a number of reasons: first, its prominence in the Canadian retail market; second, in 1991 a unionized plant sewing exclusively Alfred Sung women's wear closed, throwing 120 garment workers out of work; and third, as a result of a complicated licensing agreement for the Alfred Sung children's wear manufacturer, that company was slated to be closed just two weeks later, throwing twenty more garment workers out of work. In the place of these unionized women, the company behind Alfred Sung set up a complicated subcontracting system using homeworkers. Members of the HWA had complained that these contractors paid an extremely low piece rate, which was not enough to earn minimum wage.

16 A CA number is the registration and identification number for any consumer item sold in Canada. A manufacturer or retailer (in the case of a private label) is required to register the head office of the business as well as to label each item with its CA number. The registered information is public.

17 In June of 1993, HWA applied for funding to set up a second class on Sundays to provide two levels of English as to help some HWA members improve their skills.

18 For more information, see ILGWU and Intercede, "Meeting the Needs of Vulnerable Workers: Proposals for Improved Employment Legislation and Access to Collective Bargaining for Domestic Workers and Industrial Homeworkers," report submitted to Government of Ontario, Ministry of Labor and Ontario Women's Directorate (Toronto: ILGWU and Intercede, February 1993).

19 See Andy Banks, "The Power and Promise of Community Unionism," *Labor Research Review* 18 (1991): 17–31.

20 See *Directory of Labor Organizations in Canada* (Ottawa: Ministry of Supplies and Services, 1992). This directory includes both private-sector and public-sector workers in the nonagricultural work force. Private-sector membership has declined from 26 percent to 21 percent between 1975 and 1985 and is expected to be less than 17 percent by the mid-1990s. Moreover, private-sector unions have lost more members from permanent layoffs than they have gained by new organizing. Part of this trend is because of, and reinforced by, the shift to nonstandard and precarious employment. See J. O'Grady, "Downhill All the Way: The Labor Movement, Wage Polarization and the Wagner Act Model of Collective Bargaining" (Toronto: Centre for Research on Work and Society, 1992).

Women's Empowerment in the Making

The Philippine Bid for Social Protection

» *Lucita Lazo*

Dedicated to Aida Lava, our *kasama sa hirap a ginhawa* (companion for better or for worse) in the Filipino women's movement.

Ka Lilay weaves *sawali*, or palm leaves, for a subcontractor in her remote village in the Philippines. Her employer is a trader who subcontracts with an exporter. Once, for reasons of his own, the trader was unable to deliver on time to the exporter and could not collect his fees. He decided not to pay thirty sawali weavers who worked for him, on the pretext that their products were of poor quality. Could Ka Lilay and her coworkers have complained, filed a case in court, and had their wages paid?

Ibu Hassana has been embroidering traditional costumes in a far-flung village in Indonesia since she was twelve. Now that she is thirty-five, her eyes are blurred from her day-to-day threading and stitching. She is too poor to buy a pair of glasses, let alone consult an eye doctor. Could she ask her employer to give her glasses or to foot her doctor's bill?

THERE ARE MANY MORE SUCH CASES OF EXPLOITATION AND LEGAL INSECURITY in Thailand, Indonesia, and the Philippines. The victims are mostly women who work under subcontracting or putting-out arrangements whereby traders and middlemen, with little investment of their own, collect orders for the production of goods and assign the jobs to women who finish the goods in villages or urban slums. Their homes become extensions of factories, yet they are not part of a formal employer-employee relationship and lack the legal status of workers. As a result, home-based workers do not receive benefits extended to factory workers, such as maternity and sick leaves or medical and social insurance.

Traders and middlemen exploit homeworkers, paying low piece rates, penalizing them if they fail to deliver, and often not paying them at all for various reasons. They pass on to the workers miscellaneous costs of production, such as those of electricity, a work space and the like. Some traders make huge profits by selling at high costs to the exporters and reducing as far as they can the wages of the home-based workers. Because exporters are usually located in the cities and rely on middlemen and traders, rural homeworkers often do not know who their principal employers are and cannot make any claims upon them.

When a trader stops giving them work, some home-based workers have no choice but to produce on their own and sell directly to the market. In order to do so, they have to be able to buy raw materials and find market outlets. Many home-based workers are poor, illiterate, have no assets, and have no connections to markets or buyers. Without collateral or a guarantor they cannot borrow from banks and formal financial institutions. With little knowledge of markets and marketing, they sell only at a limited scale within their villages or to surrounding villages. Add to this their characteristic lack of self-esteem and self-confidence, and you will be hard-pressed to find homeworkers who start successful enterprises of their own.

Against this backdrop, the International Labour Organisation launched a project titled Rural Women Workers in the Putting Out System to promote the welfare of home-based women workers in rural areas in Indonesia, Thailand, and the Philippines. The dual goal of the project is to create humane, nonexploitative working conditions, at the same time making sure not to jeopardize jobs. We wanted to find ways to extend social protection to women workers without threatening their sources of income. This protection would entail increasing piece rates and wages; reducing exploitation by middlemen; reducing dependence on middlemen for job orders; providing health and other benefits, housing, and education; and providing access to and control over essential resources and social services. In countries where cheap labor is abundant, this is a tall order. Any move to increase wages or improve worker protection could mean a loss of jobs. This chapter tells the story of the rise of a homeworker movement in the Philippines. It describes which strategies worked to make homeworkers visible, which organizing techniques were successful, how the government became an ally, and what income generating interventions yielded results.

Implementing the Project

The project was the first to target home-based workers as a disadvantaged group in the Philippines. There was no established procedure on how to go about this work, and considerable preparation was necessary before we could launch practical actions. In particular, a lack of adequate data was an obstacle to project planning. We launched a series of studies to shed light on the macrocontext of homeworking in the country. The first set included an exploratory study of the working and living conditions of homeworkers, a review of policies and programs already in place, a review of laws regulating homework, and a review of organizations carrying out studies about and projects for homeworkers. A second study focused on the garment industry. It provided more specific information and formed the basis for an action program for garment homeworkers.

The studies showed that home-based workers were predominantly middle-aged women in their productive years who carried the triple burdens of housekeeping, child care, and income earning. Their husbands were farmers or laborers, and household incomes were low. Having no clearly identified employers and no written contracts, homeworkers lacked formal worker status. They generally worked long hours for low piece rates with no health insurance, occupational safety, social security, or the like.

Home-based workers were invisible to public policy-makers and were not counted in the national census and income accounts. Neither the government nor nongovernmental organizations paid attention to their conditions of work. There were no policies or programs that promoted their employment and their protection as workers. Home-based workers were covered by the Labor Code and there was some case law regarding them, though it was not very extensive. There was a roster of subcontractors at the Department of Trade and Industry but no registry of homeworkers. Legal provisions were not enforced, and there was no administrative system in place to monitor the application of labor laws to homeworkers.

There was no single organization of home-based workers that could champion their social protection and serve as a channel for development assistance. Trade unions did not deal with homeworkers, nor were they interested in taking up their cause. Home-based workers had no institutional means to voice their common concerns, influence national policy and programs, press for their rights, and redress their grievances. Except for a handful who had been educated and inspired by feminists and women activists, homeworkers were isolated, atomized, fragmented, and often unaware of the exploitative situations under which they labored.

At a first subregional technical meeting in Bangkok, Thailand, in June 1989, researchers; project staff; and representatives of governments, unions, and employer organizations, together with some homeworkers, discussed these findings and mapped out broad strategies in preparation for field actions. It became obvious that homeworkers themselves would be the most interested in changing their unfavorable situation and that it was important to mobilize, organize, and involve them in this struggle. An organization was the only answer to the comparative strength of the employers and middlemen. It would enable homeworkers to bargain with employers and give them a collective voice through which they could make themselves heard. An organization also would provide the infrastructure for channeling development aid.

But how to proceed? While the experience of the Self Employed Women's Association in Ahmedabad, India, was highly instructive, it did not provide a cut-and-dried formula. Most importantly, there was no SEWA in the Philippines, and none of the governmental agencies was concerned with home-based workers. As in other countries, the Department of Labor and the Department of Social Welfare—two likely candidates—were primarily concerned with workers in the formal sector. Which of the more than a thousand NGOs could and would be willing to take on the cause of homeworkers?

Creating an Institutional Base

After attending the technical meeting in Bangkok, a rural homeworker together with a social researcher and activist proposed to conduct systematic consultations with garment homeworkers in Bulacan province to create awareness among them. These consultations laid the groundwork for a mass organization of women homeworkers in the Philippines. From June to September 1989, 180 garment homeworkers in thirteen towns in Bulacan province attended consultation meetings, aired their grievances, identified and discussed common problems, and proposed corresponding solutions. On October 1, 1989, twenty-nine women homeworkers representing eleven provinces met in Bulacan and formed the National Network of Homeworkers or Pambansang Tagapagugnay ng mga Maggagawa sa Bahay, known by its acronym PATAMABA. This organization was a significant leap forward for the homeworkers' campaign.

The founding meeting of PATAMABA was organized at the initiative of women homeworker members of Katipunan ng Babaing Pilipina (KaBaPa), a mass-based activist nongovernmental women's organization. KaBaPa offered itself as a natural national collaborator for the ILO project. Launched on March 8, 1975, by some two thousand women, mostly from rural areas, KaBaPa today claims a membership of twenty-eight thousand women from all over the country. Many are homeworkers, some of whom have been involved in participatory action research since the early 1980s. The rural homeworker and the researcher and activist who had attended the subregional technical meeting in Bangkok and hatched the idea of conducting consultations with garment workers in Bulacan were members of KaBaPa as well.

KaBaPa seeks to promote women's equality before the law. Some specific issues dealt with by the organization include equality of economic rights, equal employment opportunities, security of employment after marriage, and equality of rights and responsibilities in the family and home. It has organized children and youth, the urban poor, and market vendors to whom it has extended solidarity during strikes and struggles against ejectment. It has carried out human resource and community development programs for rural women. KaBaPa has been most active in educating women through its indigenous training system called *gabay*. The gabays are guidelines in simple question-and-answer format to teach women how to organize, how to be good homemakers and community leaders, how to manage projects, and the like. They are written in the local dialects and have been developed over time with the grassroots participation of women. With this system, KaBaPa has trained more than twenty thousand members and nonmembers as well as five hundred trainers. Many of its projects are funded through international development aid.

The ILO launched its project on rural women in the new putting-out system in June 1988 with financial support from the Danish International Development Agency (DANIDA). Even prior to that, KaBaPa had sought assistance from the ILO office in Manila for a community-based enterprise development project by rural women. The proposal was passed on to me as the coordinator of the homeworkers' project. With minimum prodding, KaBaPa was persuaded to focus on the social protection of women workers instead of community-based enterprises as such. KaBaPa took on the role of an initiator in organizing home-based workers. It provides an institutional home for PATAMABA but envisages the homeworkers' organization developing into an independent body.

On October 21, 1989, the PATAMABA ad hoc national coordinating committee met to draft a two-year work plan covering the time span from January 1990 to December 1991. KaBaPa-PATAMABA divided the work plan into smaller subprojects to facilitate solicitation of financial support and submitted project proposals to various agencies, including the ILO-DANIDA Rural Women Homeworkers' Project, for possible funding. In January 1990, KaBaPa began its two-year Start-up Program for Educating, Training, and Organizing Women Homeworkers in the Philippines. The project sought to organize homeworkers nationwide. Specifically, KaBaPa had contacts from previous organizing in eleven regions of the country and sought to use these contacts to facilitate the initial stages of the program.[1]

Participatory Action Research as an Organizing Tool

The purpose of KaBaPa's start-up program was to improve the economic and social status of homeworkers through education, training, and organization. Specifically, the project sought to (1) select, prepare, and equip community workers and trainers for the process of organizing; (2) organize home-based workers; and (3) strengthen homeworker organizations and empower homeworkers.

A vital feature of the project's approach was the active involvement of homeworkers. With the guidance of women academics, activists, and the ILO, homeworkers codetermined the direction of their development. There were two central techniques that facilitated this approach: focused group discussions and participatory action research.

Focused group discussions served to clarify the needs of homeworkers in different geographical areas and sectors of industry, establish community profiles, and identify potential leaders and organizers. For these discussions, homeworkers assembled in small groups and, with the help of a facilitator, expressed their ideas and feelings on various issues. A community survey form drafted by KaBaPa leaders and staff from the Department of Labor and Employment's (DOLE, formerly Department of Labor) Bureau of Women and Young Workers (BWYW) aided focused group discussion. It included themes such as gender issues, working conditions, homeworkers' needs, and approaches to organizing. KaBaPa organizers conducted focused group discussions as part of their action research in eighteen provinces, involving 350 homeworkers.[2] Participatory action research was the key organizing tool. This strategy entailed training homeworkers on how to research their own situation, formulate solutions, and suggest appropriate practical actions. In the process of doing research, homeworkers would organize and raise awareness among their fellow homeworkers.

In collaboration with the Bureau of Rural Workers (BRW) of the DOLE, the University of the Philippines School for Labor and Industrial Relations (UP-SOLAIR) offered two three-day workshops on participatory action research to PATAMABA members and organizers. During these workshops, fifty homeworkers learned how to conduct such research and how to prepare video documentation. With the support of Oxfam, an international NGO, UP-SOLAIR trained another fifty homeworkers and organizers in organizing techniques. Participants in this training workshop were based in Luzon and had been identified in the course of ongoing participatory action research.

In collaboration with the UP Law Center, KaBaPa-PATAMABA designed a paralegal training program, produced gabays, and translated legal materials into Filipino to insure that homeworkers themselves could understand the law. Materials translated included the secretary of labor's paper, "The State of Jurisprudence on Homeworkers," and appropriate sections of the Labor Code. Thirty-five members of KaBaPa and PATAMABA from eleven provinces attended a paralegal orientation and training seminar from November 22 to 24, 1990, sponsored by the UP Law Center. Community organizers learned how to secure homeworkers' rights in court and how to make legal queries or speak on behalf of aggrieved women in order to obtain appropriate compensation, functions normally reserved for professional lawyers. Lawyers are expensive, and trained community organizers made legal services affordable for home-based workers.

KaBaPa also prepared six gabays on research in general, on participatory action research, on women's issues and development problems, on consciousness raising and organizing homeworkers, on factors of success and failure in organizing homeworkers, and on understanding and amending the laws affecting homeworkers' welfare. The process of developing these training materials was participatory; homeworkers related their living and working conditions, researchers provided data, and organizers shared their experiences in organizing.

KaBaPa's trainees used participatory action research as a tool of entry to organize homeworkers. Data gathered during research showed them what issues were important enough to mobilize women homeworkers in a community. Research also helped them identify potential leaders, whom they in turn trained in participatory action research. Thus, KaBaPa's training-of-trainers approach had a multiplier effect.

At the time of its first anniversary on October 1, 1990, PATAMABA had a membership of one thousand, and organizing activities were in full progress. By August 1991 it had doubled its membership to two thousand. Before its national congress in May 1991, the organization registered with the Securities and Exchange Commission, which gave it a legal personality as an organization. It also registered as a rural organization with the BRW. The network separated from KaBaPa and now exists as an independent organization, although it will continue to be supported by KaBaPa until it acquires adequate institutional capacity. Together with KaBaPa, PATAMABA drafted a five-year program, spanning from May 1991 to April 1996, to strengthen the network of homeworkers. By May 1993, PATAMABA had established chapters in twenty-two provinces.

Creating Public Awareness

Lack of public awareness was a considerable obstacle to improving the lot of homeworkers in the Philippines. To overcome this problem, we organized workshops, meetings, and dialogues that provided venues to publicly present the concerns of homeworkers to the government and other concerned agencies for the first time.

The first such meeting was a National Tripartite Workshop held in Quezon City in October 1989. Participants included representatives of the government, NGOs, worker and employer organizations, project staff, and homeworker representatives from the newly founded PATAMABA. Researchers presented findings from our initial studies, which stimulated discussion on what to do in order to alleviate the plight of homeworkers.[3] The national coordinating committee of PATAMABA had formulated a position paper at its founding meeting, which provided the basis for highly instructive contributions of homeworkers to discussions at the workshop. They used the occasion of the workshop to present the position paper to the secretary of labor and employment.

KaBaPa further sought to gain visibility for homeworkers when, upon the request of the BWYW, it took the labor undersecretary in charge of labor standards on a field trip to visit home-based papier-mâché makers in Santa Cruz, Laguna, and garment sewers in Bulacan. Shortly after this trip the undersecretary chaired the ILO Meeting of Experts on the Social Protection of Homeworkers in October 1990 in Geneva, where he played a constructive role.[4] The undersecretary's visits were featured in the Labor Department's newsletter, which is distributed in its various provincial offices.[5]

On May 1, 1991, PATAMABA convened its first national congress at the UP Law Center. At their personal expense, 172 homeworker-delegates attended the congress. They elected national officers and adopted a Declaration of Rights of Homeworkers as well as a draft of a proposed bill that they called the Magna Carta of Homeworkers. The Declaration and the bill had been drafted by participants in the paralegal orientation and training seminar half a year earlier. The national congress attracted considerable publicity.[6]

Later in May, KaBaPa-PATAMABA, with technical assistance from DOLE and financial sponsorship by the ILO; the Netherlands government; and the UP College of Social Work, Community Development, and Women's Studies, hosted a subregional workshop that served as a forum for exchanging experiences among Indonesian, Thai, and Philippine participants in the ILO-DANIDA subregional project. Thirty-four homeworkers from several provinces participated actively in the workshop as members of the Philippine delegation. The subregional workshop was also well covered by the media.[7]

All of these events fed into our media campaign. Since the subregional project was launched, PATAMABA organizers have issued a number of press releases and given numerous radio and television interviews, and the cause of homeworkers has received attention in newspapers.[8] PATAMABA has printed a brochure for distribution to a wide public that describes the homeworkers' cause and the existence of the network. With KaBaPa assistance, PATAMABA now publishes its own newsletter, called *Bahay-Ugnayan*,[9] which features articles on homework-related topics. The first issue was distributed during the national congress of homeworkers in May 1991.

Women homeworkers have diligently pursued the tasks of establishing their presence and making their voices heard by attending meetings of relevant governmental and nongovernmental organizations. They have participated in conferences on women's health and the environment as well as meetings of the interagency Committee on Labor, Income, and Employment Statistics. Through the latter they helped pave the way for homeworkers' visibility by supporting the Labor Department's effort to include homeworkers as a category of workers in the national census and in household surveys.

Making the Government an Ally

Immediately after the subregional workshop in May 1991, some Philippine participants formed a National Steering Committee that formalized governmental and nongovernmental collaboration in the homeworkers' campaign. The committee is an interagency ad hoc group, cochaired by PATAMABA and created as a national instrument for handling homeworkers' concerns in the absence of a defined responsible government office. It initiates links with officials of governmental and nongovernmental agencies to ensure that the views of homeworkers are heard and their interests promoted. It is hoped that the committee will facilitate homeworkers' access to resources and services.

With the creation of the National Steering Committee, homeworkers have in effect gained official recognition. Government support for their cause has never been as evident and positive as during the past few years. Although constraints in the government's resources and priorities stand in the way of a vigorous promotion of homeworkers' welfare, there have been significant, concrete steps forward. For example, the BRW of DOLE has created a committee to review laws and recommend changes taking into account the needs of women homeworkers. It has created a small homeworker support unit to handle issues relating to homework, and, together with the BWYW, it has functioned as a focal point for activities on homework.

Several such activities have been initiated. In cooperation with KaBaPa, the BRW sponsored a seminar on participatory action research for women homeworkers from selected rural areas nationwide. The BRW conducted a nationwide survey of homeworkers which has become the basis for policy recommendations and actions. In 1994, the ministry of labor and employment extended a grant of 3 million pesos for homeworkers' socioeconomic programs. The government welcomed KaBaPa as the women's sector representative in the intersectoral committee that updated the medium-term development plan for the Philippines. The matter of promoting homeworkers' welfare was included in the plan, particularly in the section on social welfare and community development. The plan calls for enforcing laws on homework and clarifying the welfare benefits of homeworkers such as Social Security insurance.

On the initiative of PATAMABA, a representative of the Social Security System (SSS), has made contact with homeworkers and has advised them on how to become SSS members and draw benefits. SSS representatives attended the subregional workshop in May 1991, where they learned about and realized the need for social protection of women homeworkers. SSS is also a member of the National Steering Committee.

DOLE has worked with PATAMABA on the issue of new legislation. DOLE considered the Magna Carta that homeworkers passed at their national congress and recommended that enforcement of existing legislation be given priority over creating a new law. DOLE also suggested that it will formulate new rules and regulations to implement provisions of the Labor Code pertaining to subcontracting. Homeworkers were persuaded by DOLE's arguments and have shelved the Magna Carta for the time being.

Socioeconomic Assistance

Improving the material welfare of homeworkers was a major goal of the ILO-DANIDA project and remains the ultimate aspiration of the homeworkers' campaign. While collective improvements in wages, social security benefits, health, and safety have yet to materialize, there have been successes with socioeconomic assistance to particular communities. For example, in Barrio San Francisco in the province of Bulacan, twenty-five women homeworkers received a grant from the ILO-DANIDA project in early 1989. The homeworkers were members of a garments cooperative that they had formed to "fight subcontractors who exploit garment sewers and to awaken communities on the plight of homeworkers."[10] They used the grant as seed money to set up a workshop. About 28,000 pesos were applied as working capital and 20,000 pesos kept in the bank for future use. The women also agreed to set aside 25 percent of their net profit for a revolving fund. The workshop is located in the dwelling house of their manager, Ka Ester. Beneath her house is a cement space with wooden walls that houses six sewing machines. This space is well ventilated, but lighting could be improved. Women come to the workshop at about ten o'clock in the morning and begin their sewing. They interrupt their work to go back home and cook meals. After lunch, they return and continue work until about five o'clock in the afternoon. At that time, they return home to cook dinner.

Forming the cooperative has brought its members into direct contact with the market and awakened their consciousness of market forces. The products of the cooperative have had a slow turnover. Cooperative members recognize that they need to upgrade the quality of their products. They know they have to acquire or rent an edging machine to make their inside hems look neater. Exporters, whom they contacted through KaBaPa, told them that the quality of their products leaves much to be desired.

The women have also learned about the importance of timing in building their enterprise. They noted that their raw materials would have been cheaper had they launched production earlier. When their products entered the market during the Christmas season, other producers had already flooded the market with similar products. Some women have had to accept sewing jobs outside their cooperative to fill in the slack time. But the cooperative has also shifted to rice trading during periods when the garments market is slack and has made some profit buying and selling rice.

PATAMABA administers a revolving fund obtained under the ILO-DANIDA project and provides one-year loans at a below-market rate of 15 percent. It has funded projects of homeworkers who have been organized in Cebu, Bicol Region, CALABAR Zone, and Central and Northern Luzon. Projects seek to secure livelihoods and generate incomes by providing credit, forming cooperatives and microenterprises.

Limited resources have circumscribed ILO-DANIDA project actions within a very limited scale and scope. However, KaBaPa has been able to receive funds and generate a pool of resources for its homework-related projects from other donors, such as the governments of the Netherlands, Canada, and the United States. Such funds have enabled KaBaPa to embark on various development projects that benefit homeworkers.

Conclusion

The main thrust of the ILO-DANIDA field actions in the Philippines was to focus on nationwide organizing. This goal rested on the assumption that women could remedy their exploitation and ameliorate sweatshop working conditions if they had a voice and collective strength. Organizing became the all-encompassing cause of the women activists of KaBaPa. During a field visit to project sites, an evaluation mission found a high degree of awareness among homeworkers regarding the importance of organizing, so one central project goal has been achieved.

The mission also found that homeworkers knew little about access to resources such as credit and marketing and felt that there was a need to strengthen socioeconomic assistance. KaBaPa's focus on organizing was also

built on the expectation that homeworker organizations could become a channel for providing socioeconomic aid. It remains to be seen whether organizing
will translate into an improvement of the economic situation of homeworkers.

Notes

I wish to acknowledge the support of my colleagues at the ILO Geneva and Bangkok;
our donors from DANIDA; the cooperation of Undersecretary Cresenciano Trajano
of the Philippine Department of Employment; Rosalinda Pineda-Ofreneo of the
University of the Philippines; Ka Trining, Ka Lyn, and Ka Gilda of KaBaPa; Ka Ester
and the women of PATAMABA; and the many unnamed women and men who helped
us in the endeavor to give birth to a "homeworkers' movement" in the Philippines and
who are still with us in the struggle.

1   The following provinces were involved: Isabela, Cagayan, Pangasinan, Bulacan,
    Pampanga, Bataan, Tarlac, Nueva Ecija, Rizal, La Union, Metro Manila, Laguna,
    Batangas, Quezon, Cavite, Albay, Sorsogon, Negros, Cebu, Sulu, Lanao, and
    Sultan Kudarat.

2   Focused group discussions identified the following homeworking activities as
    typical for various provinces: Sewing in Isabela; sewing and embroidery in Rizal;
    sewing, papier-mâché work, weaving, and making wooden toys in Laguna;
    sewing, embroidery, and stitching sequins and decor onto garments in Bulacan;
    sewing and broomstick making in Nueva Ecija; sewing in Batangas; sewing and
    handicrafts in Metro Manila; weaving *tikiw* (a variety of local fiber used for
    weaving bags) in Pampanga; weaving fans and baskets in Quezon; sewing, hat and
    bag weaving, and crocheting in Camarines Sur; clay jar making in Tarlac; bamboo
    craft in Pangasinan; rattan craft in Mandawe City; and weaving *baetong* (a variety
    of local fiber) in Bataan.

3   The proceedings have been published in Lucita Lazo, ed., *Homeworkers in Southeast
    Asia: The Struggle for Social Protection in the Philippines* (Bangkok: International
    Labour Organisation, Regional Office for Asia and the Pacific, 1992).

4   The meeting brought together experts from governments, unions, and employer
    organizations around the world to advise the ILO on how to improve the situation
    of homeworkers.

5   "Homeworkers Vulnerable to Abuses, Insecurities," and "Home Is Where the
    Work Is," *Philippine Labor* (Manila) 16 (October 1990): 2, 8–9.

6   "Asian Homeworkers Meet in RP May 10," *News Today* (Manila), May 1, 1991, p.
    3; "Homeworkers as Exploited Class," *Businessworld* (Manila), May 1, 1991, p. 8
    and in *Philippine Daily Inquirer* (Manila), May 17, 1991.

7   "Homeworkers Meet On," *Manila Bulletin* (Manila), May 7,1991, p. 5; "8M
    Home-Based Workers Grossly Underpaid: DOLE," *Malaya* (Manila), May 13,
    1991, p. 2; "Homeworkers: An Exploited Lot," *Malaya* (Manila), May 10, 1991, p.
    18; "Homeworkers' Aid Sought," *Manila Bulletin* (Manila), May 13, 1991, p. 16;

"Laws to Protect Home-Based Workers Sought," *Manila Bulletin* (Manila), May 19, 1991, p. 12.

8 A selection of articles are: "DOLE Pushes Legislation for Homeworkers," *Businessworld* (Manila), April 10, 1991, p. 11; "Drilon Appeals for Welfare of Homeworkers," *The Manila Chronicle* (Manila), October 7, 1989, p. 3; "Drilon Wants Protection for 7M Home Workers," *Businesworld* (Manila) 9 October 1989, p. 11; "Drilon Vows to Protect Homeworkers," *Manila Bulletin* (Manila), October 7, 1989, pp. 1, 20; "Gov't, NGOs Help Homeworkers," *News Today* (Manila), October 6, 1989, p. 3; "Help for Homeworkers Sought," *The New Chronicle* (Manila), April 10, 1991, p. 4; "Homeworkers Organise to Get Better Income," *Daily Globe* (Manila), January 16, 1990, p. 14; "Homeworkers Widely Ignored Despite GDP Contribution," *Philippine Labor* (Manila), March 1991, p. 7; "It's Worth a Try," *Philippine Daily Inquirer* (Manila), October 7, 1989, p. 8; "ILO Cites Gov't, NGO Efforts to Promote Homeworking," *Businessworld* (Manila), April 29, 1991, p. 12; "Look After Homeworkers' Weal, Drilon Asks Solons," *Daily Globe* (Manila), October 7, 1989, p. 6; "The Most Exploited Women Workers," *People's Journal* (Manila), October 7, 1989.

9 Literally translates as "Home for Linking."

10 "Success Story: Garments Cooperative," report presented at the ILO Sub-regional Workshop on Homeworkers, May 7–10, 1991, Manila, Philippines.

15 »

Making Links
The Growth of Homeworker Networks

« *Jane Tate*

AT A MAY 1990 CONFERENCE IN THE NETHERLANDS, PEOPLE WORKING WITH
homeworkers from a number of different countries met and discussed their
experiences. Ela Bhatt spoke about the Self Employed Women's Association,
in Ahmedabad, India, an independent women's trade union of which she is
general secretary. Lucita Lazo, the coordinator of a program in Southeast Asia,
explained ongoing research and action on behalf of homeworkers in the
Philippines, Thailand, and Indonesia. Other speakers from the South worked
with Palestinian women in refugee camps and outworkers in Hong Kong.
Homeworkers and project workers from Britain and the Netherlands talked
about their work, and speakers from France, Germany, and Belgium described
policies on homeworking in their countries. Other participants were
researchers or represented international organizations. One key recommen-
dation of the conference was that international and regional networks should
be established as a way in which those active with homeworkers in different
countries and continents could maintain contact and communicate with each
other as well as act jointly at the international level.[1]

This desire to maintain and build contacts with other groups grew out of a
number of common themes that emerged at the conference. The experience

and nature of homework is similar whether it takes place in industrialized or developing countries. Everywhere the majority of homeworkers are women, and many of them are the main earners in their households. Yet their paid work in the home is generally invisible and not acknowledged as "real work" or "a proper job." Pay and conditions for homeworkers are generally inferior to those of office or factory workers, and homeworkers are often outside any form of regulation; even if regulation exists, the work takes place in an informal manner. In many different parts of the world homework is on the increase and is often found at the end of international and national subcontracting chains. Because homework has so many common features worldwide, it makes sense to coordinate campaigns to improve wages and working conditions through better legislation at regional and international levels, through rules created by the European Union or through standard-setting by the International Labour Organisation. How to draw up legislation was one of the main discussion points at the Netherlands conference.

Legislation will not necessarily improve conditions for homeworkers unless they are organized. But how to organize a scattered work force? Successful practice from different parts of the world has proved inspirational. At the conference, the experience of SEWA in organizing women workers in the informal sector in India was one such example. Another was that of the Australian Clothing and Allied Trades Union. In many places, such as the Netherlands and Britain, the initiative to work with homeworkers has come from community-based women's groups. They often have trade union support but without day-to-day involvement on the part of organized labor. Their focus is local work, developing contact and trust with homeworkers, and they do not have large organizations behind them to build international links. The opportunity to meet and learn from each other thus has proved invaluable.

Before the Netherlands conference, contact had existed between different groups. In fact, such contact was a prerequisite for the meeting. But the conference was the first occasion in which people came together from both North and South and where homeworkers themselves, as well as representatives from projects and trade unions met with researchers and representatives from international bodies. Four years later, in March 1994, another meeting occurred in Brussels to take the first steps in setting up the international network discussed at the earlier conference. Many of the same organizations attended as well as new groups.

This chapter considers international meetings and visits from the perspective of one local group, the West Yorkshire Homeworking Unit in Britain. It is not intended to be a comprehensive record, as there have been many meetings besides those that we know of or have participated in. The account will show

how these links have developed at a number of levels and require further development into a wider network.

West Yorkshire Homeworking Unit

In 1988, a group of women drawn from local community organizations, the voluntary sector, and church organizations convened a conference on homeworking in Bradford in the North of England. The aim was to initiate work to improve the conditions of homeworking in the area. We set up an institution, the West Yorkshire Homeworking Unit, and began to publish information for homeworkers and build contacts with local women. In 1990, the Unit employed its first outreach workers and in 1992, held another conference attended by over sixty area homeworkers. This second conference marked an important step in the development of the Unit in that it focused on the active participation of homeworkers, mainly from West Yorkshire but also from other parts of Britain. Significantly, it also included international delegates from homework groups in India, Portugal, and the Netherlands.

The main aim of the Unit always has been to work locally with homeworkers in West Yorkshire. But from its early days, it belonged to a network of similar groups in Britain. The Leicester Outwork Campaign (LOC) made a major contribution to the initial conference. LOC has sought to empower homeworkers since its founding in the early 1980s, and its members held many valuable ideas about how to work with homeworkers and what could be achieved. The Unit also has taken part in the National Group on Homeworking and the Northern Region Homeworking Campaign, which has established links among different projects and officers working with homeworkers across the North of England. These contacts have provided a source of support and ideas as well as practical help with publications and material relevant to homeworkers.

Homeworker support groups around England have used a variety of innovative tools to reach homeworkers which the West Yorkshire Unit has adopted. We have produced Fact Packs, distributed free of charge to homeworkers, which contain information on employment rights and welfare benefits and addresses of unions, homeworker advocacy groups, and other grassroots organizations that provide support and assist with grievances. We distribute a newsletter with articles in several languages (Punjabi, Gujarati, Bengali, Chinese, and Urdu, in addition to English) and operate a hotline that homeworkers can call for information and support. We often follow up calls from homeworkers with visits to their homes so they can get to know us and we can tell them about our work. We organize weekend outings to the sea that allow homeworkers to emerge from their isolation. These outings are extremely popular and have attracted many new members. When we have business meetings, we offer child care and transportation where possible. We also try to provide homeworkers with an allowance for lost earnings. In many ways, these strategies have more in common with community organizing than with factory organizing. Homeworker advocacy groups throughout Britain have relied on these techniques.

Direct Links

The Unit made contact with homeworker advocates in the Netherlands at an early stage of its development. The Dutch Women's Union, part of the Dutch Trade Union Confederation (FNV), has played a central role in efforts to improve the situation of homeworkers. This unusual union organizes all women, whether in paid employment or not, and has played an important bridging role between homework projects and the trade union movement as a whole. In the early 1980s, the Women's Union conducted a survey of its membership and found over one hundred different kinds of paid work being done in the home. After this survey, union members visited the Leicester Outwork Campaign and used some of LOC's ideas to establish projects in the Netherlands.[2]

Following discussions with people from these homework projects, a delegation of homeworkers from West Yorkshire visited their counterparts in the Netherlands. Eight women, most of them homeworkers, traveled to Homework Support Centers, the Women's Union, and other related groups in a four-day visit organized by Hanka Heumakers, who was then at the National Homework Center in Hengelo. They exchanged experiences at meetings with staff from the support centers and other homeworkers, describing their own work, its advantages and disadvantages, and future plans. They visited homeworkers and talked to them about their work: heat-sealing packets, binding books, clothing and leather work, and word processing. (The West Yorkshire delegation itself had knowledge of a wide range of homeworking: clothing, print work, white-collar services, electronics, and knitting.)

The visit was valuable in broadening women's understanding of their own experience. Many homeworkers suffer from depression and stress as a result of isolation and feelings of powerlessness in the face of low pay and poor working conditions. Even when relatively well paid, their isolation often leads them to believe that their problems are private or personal. Talking to women in another country, whose experiences closely matched their own, served as a strategy to develop self-confidence and feelings of solidarity. Seeing the work of the Homework Support Centers also gave them ideas on how they could organize in West Yorkshire. The homeworkers particularly noted the strength local projects derived from the support of a national organization, the Women's Union.[3]

At the level of grassroots exchanges between homeworkers, the Bradford conference of July 1992 was an important step for the West Yorkshire Homeworking Unit. Not only did many homeworkers actively participate but there were international delegations from the Netherlands, Portugal, and India. The conference consisted mainly of small workshops so that women felt free to talk about their work, the problems they faced, and their hopes and aspirations for the future. Members of the three delegations from other countries outlined their experience of working with homeworkers in plenary sessions. Ranjan Desai and Jetun Pathan from SEWA made a deep impression when speaking on SEWA's years of experience. Jetun was herself a homeworker, sewing waste cloth from the mills into quilt covers; now she is a SEWA organizer. She recounted how SEWA had organized the quilt makers and garment workers and how they had struggled for recognition as workers, patiently building up their strength and using different means, such as demonstrations and sit-ins, to insist on their legal rights. Ranjan spoke mainly about the cooperatives SEWA initiated to bring together self-employed women and increase their earning power. SEWA is particularly proud of its women's bank, which extends low-interest loans to self-employed women workers.

The two European groups presented different strategies. In the Netherlands, the basic approach has been to set up advice and support centers for homeworkers and, at the same time, to campaign for a law regulating homework while encouraging unions to organize homeworkers. The women from Portugal talked of their long struggle to establish a cooperative and, in one case, an independent business.[4] As well as the conference, the Unit organized visits and meetings for the delegates from other countries. These meetings enabled the women from abroad to understand more about conditions in Britain as well as allowing them to speak to a wider audience.

The next year, three homeworkers from West Yorkshire, together with one of the outreach workers, visited Portugal.[5] Such direct exchanges among grassroots organizations and homeworkers themselves are most important because they offer a means of empowering homeworkers. The West Yorkshire Homeworking Unit views these personal exchanges as a way to share experiences and build homeworker knowledge. This knowledge in turn feeds back into the development of activities in West Yorkshire. The inspiration for setting up a homeworkers' association in West Yorkshire came, after all, from the experience of SEWA. After homeworkers had heard of its work with women in Ahmedabad, they were inspired to try to establish a similar organization in Britain. The West Yorkshire Homeworking Unit has always stressed the need to involve homeworkers themselves in working out solutions to the problems they face rather than speaking or acting on their behalf. However, contacts have had to happen without any formal organization linking different projects and without abundant funds.

Other Links

The West Yorkshire Homeworking Unit has always worked with an alliance of different organizations, mainly in the voluntary sector. An independent voluntary association and a church group jointly manage the Unit. In many local areas the Unit collaborates with other kinds of organizations, reflecting the different needs of homeworkers and various strategies to improve their situation. It works with training agencies to develop programs for homeworkers and encourages individual homeworkers to develop skills and formal qualifications. Since homework is often hidden and rarely spoken about, the Unit creates links with local community workers who have built trust and confidence with women in different communities. Where it can, the Unit works with trade unions in efforts to improve pay and conditions for homeworkers through union membership and collective bargaining.

The Unit also accumulates information on homework. Official records in Britain fail to include most homework because homeworkers are rarely registered and employers are often reluctant to talk about their use of them. As a result, most information comes from homeworkers themselves. Hence, researchers who are studying women's employment or particular sectors of industry, such as clothing, often ask the Unit for information. A number of these research contacts have generated international links.

Church-sponsored urban or industrial missions have provided another source of grassroots contact in Europe. A member of the West Yorkshire Homeworking Unit has been active in these networks. Although these groups do not deal directly with homeworking, they are concerned with issues of poverty, economic justice, and the "marginalization" of workers. This concern opens the way to raising the issue of homework, particularly because a high proportion of homeworkers in the North of Europe are from black and migrant communities.[6] This network led to contacts with homeworkers in Portugal. Other opportunities have included homeworker participation in a World Council of Churches conference on the growing divide between the rich and poor and discussions in Germany on the issue of homework.

Voluntary organizations concerned with issues relating to women and work or focused on different industries have offered another source of international contact. The Industrial Restructuring Education Network Europe (IRENE) organized the Netherlands conference. IRENE is a Europewide educational body that arranges meetings on industrial restructuring and brings together researchers, trade unionists, and activists from the North and South. Some of its other events, although not directly focused on homeworking, consider related issues, for example, the clothing and electronics industries.

Similarly, the Clean Clothes Campaign in the Netherlands concerns itself with issues of employment in the clothing industry worldwide. It promotes a Fair Trade Charter, which, if accepted by retailers, would guarantee decent pay and conditions from the top to the bottom of the production chain, including homeworkers. A key aspect of this campaign is building links with workers' groups in different parts of the world in order to effectively monitor production of clothing. The campaign has always included homeworkers as an important segment of the work force. The Center for Research on Multinational Corporations—know by its Dutrch acronym as SOMO—is another independent organization in Amsterdam connected to homeworking campaigns which has carried out valuable research on the clothing industry.[7]

The West Yorkshire Homeworking Unit has also worked closely with the British group Women Working Worldwide. This group has a project, based in the North of England, that focuses on women in the textile and garment industry. Because the concerns of our organizations overlap, we have been able to collaborate and supplement each other's research and campaigning. An educational pack produced by Women Working Worldwide, for example, included material on homeworkers collected by the Unit.[8]

Most contacts among these different organizations have developed on an informal basis and form a loose network, mainly of women, working on related issues. Contacts develop at meetings and conferences and are followed up in a relatively unorganized way. A fruitful exchange of information and research occurs, but limited resources restrict the extent of such contacts.

Research

Both the West Yorkshire Homeworking Unit and the National Group on Homeworking have always had close links with researchers. In West Yorkshire, a study by Bradford University helped to establish the need for work with homeworkers. The National Group on Homeworking has always encouraged active participation by researchers on homeworking or related fields. The local projects, in turn, have often collaborated with researchers who needed contacts with homeworkers. Such research has also proven to be an important area for international connections. Researchers Sheila Rowbotham and Swasti Mitter took up the global dimensions of homework with the World Institute for Development Economics Research (WIDER), the United Nations University in Helsinki.[9] In December 1991, the Association of Women in Development conference in Washington provided another opportunity to meet and discuss a strategy for working together internationally.

This conference again brought together a range of people including researchers, trade unionists, and organizers working with homeworkers in practical action programs. It included organizations and individuals from the United States, India, Southeast Asia, the Netherlands, and Britain who had been represented at the conference in the Netherlands and others working in similar areas, as well as representatives of trade unions: the International Ladies' Garment Workers Union and, on the level of international trade secretariats, the International Textile, Garment, and Leather Workers' Federation (ITGLWF). Sessions established once again the many common threads linking the situation of homeworkers in different countries around the world as well as their connections to other areas of women's work. They also presented different examples of organization among women. Renana Jhabvala, SEWA's secretary, updated the activities of the Indian organization. Lucita Lazo outlined the program that she coordinates in Southeast Asia. Researchers presented their findings on homework in Pakistan and Iran. Women from Uganda and Egypt discussed labor law reform and its impact on women and spoke about unpaid family work. I presented the campaigns of the West Yorkshire Homeworking Unit. Susan Cowell from the ILGWU, New York, talked about her union's Campaign for Justice. Although this campaign did not organize homeworkers, it did represent a broad approach to organizing within the clothing industry that included the entire production chain and involved a range of organizations other than the union. This approach meant working closely with community-based groups from which the clothing workers came as well as promoting the "union label" idea with consumer organizations. A final session at this conference considered the need for an international network to ensure communication and coordination among the different groups working with homeworkers around the world. It was proposed that initial attempts should be made to establish the network in Europe but that it would be necessary to set up regional centers.

The International Labour Organisation

The ILO has been another source of contacts and exchanges for people concerned with homeworking. SEWA has fought a long campaign over the past twenty years through official trade union channels for the recognition of home-based workers and for their inclusion in the debates and programs of the ILO. It has campaigned for the ILO to establish a convention on homework that would set international standards to regulate pay and conditions.

In October 1990, the ILO held an Expert Meeting on this issue. This tripartite discussion involved experts from governments, trade unions, and employer organizations. Visitors and observers were also present, with the latter permitted to participate in the discussion. The West Yorkshire Homeworking Unit sent a visitor to the meeting as a representative of the National Group on Homeworking in Britain. This meeting was a valuable experience for us in understanding the workings of international organizations such as the ILO. It also provided an opportunity to make new contacts with homeworker groups, particularly from Japan, as well as renew older contacts.

Attendees of the Expert Meeting did not agree on the need for an international standard on homework and recommended that the ILO's Governing Body "weigh the importance of the issues involved in order to decide on appropriate action."[10] The Governing Body put the issue on the agenda of the 1995 annual meeting of ILO member states. As part of the preparations for this conference, in 1994 the ILO distributed questionnaires to governments asking for their responses to a proposed convention and their recommendations on homework. This process has prompted further coordination between homeworking groups and between them and trade unions in preparing responses for individual governments.

The ILO also has undertaken significant research and "technical" programs on homework in countries of the South. These programs have included regional seminars and exchanges between program participants from India and Southeast Asia. The program on homework in three countries of Southeast Asia holds regular workshops at which delegations from participating countries meet and share experiences. Although activities around homework must be developed to suit conditions in each country, participants have found exchanging experiences to be extremely important.[11] The programs have also included visits to other countries, particularly visits designed to help workers learn from the experience of SEWA. Although some of these exchanges have existed at an organizational level, they have also included fellowships for individual homeworkers. In 1992, two homeworkers from Chiangmai in northern Thailand visited SEWA on a fellowship. Cloth weaver Warin Guntakan explored the work of SEWA with women weaving at home. Duangduen Kamchai, who works with bamboo and reed, gained inspiration from SEWA's development of social insurance for its members.

The West Yorkshire Homeworking Unit has been able to further its contacts in Southeast Asia by taking part in two of the subregional workshops. The first of these was in Manila, the Philippines, in May 1991 and the second in Malang, Indonesia, in December 1993. In both workshops, Lucita Lazo, the coordinator of the regional program, included sessions with people from outside the region talking about their work with homeworkers. In addition to the formal workshop, these meetings provided opportunities to visit homeworkers in the field. In 1991, members of PATAMABA, the homeworkers' network in the Philippines, brought Hanka Heumakers and me to the countryside. We went into villages where women performed many different kinds of homework, both industrial clothing and craft work. In 1993, I was also able to visit craft homeworkers in Chiangmai and garment homeworkers in a district of Bangkok, Thailand. These contacts have been important for the West Yorkshire Homeworking Unit because they have contributed to an understanding of homework in an international context, including the growing internationalization of the economy. The same retailers who buy homeworker-made clothing in the Philippines may also buy goods from manufacturers who employ homeworkers in Europe.

At another level, homeworker organizations in Asia—SEWA, PATAMABA, and Homenet, the homeworkers' network in northern Thailand—offer inspiration to homeworkers in Europe. In March 1994, Lucita Lazo visited West Yorkshire and spoke at a meeting where she showed a video on Homenet. She also met with homeworkers in Leeds. Lucita talked about activities in Thailand, the Philippines, and Indonesia, and attendees concerned with cooperative work were struck by the common themes and problems women face in different parts of the world. This subject was even more strongly developed through the participation in the meeting of Ntokozo Mbhele from the Association for the Establishment of the Self Employed Women's Union in Durban, South Africa, who spoke of the association's experience in establishing a union for women workers in the informal sector.

In mid-1994, the West Yorkshire Homeworking Unit discussed another way of establishing links: Homeworkers who were having difficulty finding work explored the possibility of setting up a cooperative business. They began to consider creating a fair trade link through a direct connection with the homeworkers' network in Thailand. They would import goods produced by Thai homeworkers and sell them directly to customers in England, thus eliminating exporters and intermediaries.

The ILO programs in Asia have provided useful insight on how work could be developed at the level of the EU. The ILO, like the EU, is responsible for coordinating programs and providing "technical" help. Funding comes from development organizations or foreign aid agencies in Western countries, such as Denmark and Finland. The programs operate at a number of different levels, including grassroots organizations, voluntary associations, and government bodies. This structure provides a useful model for those of us attempting to build a European network, as will be outlined below.

"Unions" for Homeworkers

Homeworkers require a more flexible organizing approach than workers concentrated in a discrete space. In addition, they need to be addressed as *women* workers. SEWA probably has the most extensive experience in organizing home-based workers. Set up in the early 1970s, originally as part of the textile union, it organizes women workers in the informal sector, including home-based workers. Among these women, there are two basic groups: pieceworkers who work for an employer, for example garment machining, and own-account workers who produce crafts, such as baskets or woven goods. SEWA has become well known internationally because it has succeeded in doing what many thought was impossible: organizing women in the informal sector. Although it employs multiple strategies, ranging from trade unionism to cooperatives and social service provisions, SEWA has adhered to a basic message: empowering women through their own organization. Clearly, conditions in other parts of the world may be very different from those in Ahmedabad, but SEWA's message of the need to organize and its practical example have relevance for many groups of laboring women, including homeworkers.

This relevance was demonstrated when SEWA members contributed to the West Yorkshire Homeworking Unit conference of July 1992. SEWA has had many regional and international contacts over the years. One recent example is the Association for the Establishment of the Self Employed Women's Union, which was set up in Durban, South Africa, in 1993. This pilot project resulted directly from a visit by organizers to SEWA. The association has now successfully launched the Self Employed Women's Union (SEWU) with over 250 members. Because of the different conditions in South Africa, SEWU will not be a direct copy of SEWA in India but will develop in its own directions and act as an inspiration for other groups in its region. International contact has led to this kind of exchange of ideas and inspiration. Though usually organized on a bilateral basis, such exchanges should be multilateral. There is an evident need for an international network that could spread successful experiences more widely.

As an official trade union registered in Gujarat, SEWA has played its key role through the international trade union movement, working with international trade secretariats and federations to win recognition for home-based workers. A membership of over fifty thousand women workers brings considerable influence. SEWA's success has inspired a broader vision of trade unionism than is common in industrialized countries. Historically, industrial unions in the West have concentrated on large factories that bring together hundreds or thousands of workers, the majority of whom are men. This practice has been difficult to adapt to organizing women workers, particularly homeworkers, who are scattered over a wide area and are often invisible in comparison to a factory-based work force.

Over the last century, Western trade unions have fought for bans on homework, seeing it as a threat to organized workers, as a form of cheap labor that is intrinsically exploitative. Beginning in the 1970s, there has been a shift in trade union policy on homework, and many now advocate the organization of homeworkers and their inclusion in union membership. Although it is a step forward, this change did not in itself answer the question of how homeworkers could be organized. The main difficulty has always been that homeworkers risk losing their work by organizing because it can easily be moved to other groups of homeworkers if one group makes demands on employers.

SEWA's way of organizing responds to the needs of its women members. It supplements traditional unionization with other strategies, such as the development of cooperatives, provision of services such as child minding and medical care, extension of low-interest credit, and training courses. These new methods of organizing are particularly relevant at a time when the economy in industrialized countries is being restructured and many trade unions are having to look again at the ways they operate. The restructuring of economies has meant a growing number of women in the work force, many of them working parttime on a casual or temporary basis. Women compose the majority of the flexible work force, of which homeworkers are one extreme.

Industrial restructuring led to growth of homework, particularly in industries such as clothing, leather, and electronics. Whereas many people thought of homework as an old-fashioned form of production that would gradually die out, a different trend is actually taking place. For example, the Australian Clothing and Allied Trades Union launched a campaign to unionize the growing number in its industry, who outnumbered those working in factories.[12] Before the union began this campaign, organizers visited homeworking groups in Britain, Italy, and Switzerland to learn from their experiences, demonstrating again the importance of international contacts.

Homeworking groups in Britain have had general support from the trade unions since the 1980s. At a local level, many projects have union support and there have been some practical examples of joint work. The West Yorkshire Homeworking Unit has also had some contact over the years with the ILGWU in Toronto, which has developed extensive programs for homeworkers in the clothing industry. Before launching its campaign, as described by Alex Dagg in Chapter 13 of this volume, the union collected material about other homeworking projects, particularly those in Britain. It has since developed the work in Canada at a number of different levels, including setting up the Homeworkers' Association as part of the union structure and conducting a "clean clothes" campaign on the Amsterdam model. Along with international delegates from the United States, Mexico, and Nicaragua, two members of the West Yorkshire Homeworking Unit attended a November 1992 conference sponsored by the Association in Toronto.[13] The exchange of publications and research, as well as informal and formal visits, has maintained bilateral contact between the Toronto association and the Unit.

Europe

International contacts have been important to the West Yorkshire Home-working Unit in providing many examples of flexible ways to organize women workers through trade unions or other groups that seek to empower women. Examples from the South have often proven particularly useful. In spite of very different conditions, many of the approaches of Southern organizations were relevant to women in Europe. We have also tried to develop a regional network within the EU and to draw on the resources of the European Commission.

From 1992 to 1993, the Commission funded and convened a Working Group on Homeworking that brought together a number of experts from different countries in Europe. The aim was to compare existing information, drawing on both official and unofficial sources. Participants included labor department officials, employer and trade union representatives, staffs of homeworker projects, researchers, members of IRENE, and staff members of the Commission. The resulting report compiled diverse information on homeworking in Europe. As with other research, information had to be drawn from a range of sources. This information is uneven with few "hard" statistics. Nonetheless, the report established that homework has been growing in Europe as the restructuring of economies has taken place. Enough is known to establish that pay and conditions do not meet regulations, or at best are inferior to those for factory workers, and that the majority of homeworkers are women. In northern Europe, homework is extensive both in indigenous and in black and other minority communities. The Commission published the report in nine languages; the report helped to publicize the issues and to make homeworking more visible.[14]

Participation in the Working Group on Homeworking enabled the West Yorkshire Homeworking Unit to build new contacts with people in southern Europe. These contacts were made mainly through a researcher from Greece, Dina Vaiou, who was a member of the group and who, as part of a team, had done extensive research on the local economy in Thessaloniki in northern Greece. The economy of this area depended on chains of subcontracting that often ended with homeworkers in a variety of industries: clothing, electronics, engineering, toys, and plastics. These findings convinced Greek trade unionists that homeworking was an important factor in their industries. Our network expanded to include researchers doing similar work in Italy and Spain, who have enabled us to begin building contacts in these countries as well.

Following publication of the Working Group on Homeworking's report, the Commission organized a seminar to discuss its findings in March 1994. This seminar was an official event, bringing together representatives of national governments, trade unions, and employer organizations as well as homeworkers and representatives of homeworkers' groups. Other participants included officials from the ILO, who explained their programs on homework, and representatives of groups working with homeworkers outside Europe. Through the seminar, we developed further grassroots connections. Dina Vaiou made contact with women trade unionists actively involved in setting up a project to organize homeworkers in Greece. The member of the working group from Portugal got in touch with a trade union in Madeira, an autonomous region, which had a long history of organizing women home embroiderers. A delegation from Italy included women who had actively worked with homeworkers in the leather industry near Pisa and others carrying out research for a union with homeworkers in a range of industries.

The contributions of homeworkers and organizers at the seminar were important in bringing the report to life. They were backed up by videos and slides that provided a concrete portrait of what homework entailed and some of the activities going on among homeworkers. Participants emphasized the possibilities for organizing homeworkers not only in Europe, but throughout the world, with Meena Patel talking about the work of SEWA, Alex Dagg explaining the activities of her union in Canada, and Lucita Lazo outlining the ILO program in Southeast Asia. Speakers from the ILO stressed the international nature of homework, underlined common lessons from the various programs, and emphasized the importance of the upcoming discussion on homework at the 1995 International Labour Conference.

A European Homeworking Group emerged out of this seminar. Its members were people actively working with homeworkers through trade unions, churches, or community organizations. Initially consisting of people from the Netherlands, Portugal (including Madeira), Greece, and the United Kingdom, the group extended to include Germany, Spain, Italy, and France in the course of the year. The group aimed to establish channels of communication and ways of exchanging experience and to set up a European homeworking network. It obtained funding for 1994, and held three meetings in Thessaloniki, Northern Greece; Bradford, West Yorkshire, United Kingdom; and Pisa, Italy. This enabled members of the group to visit homeworkers and meet people concerned with homeworking, including trade unionists, employers, local authority officers, and members.

At these international meetings, people exchanged experiences on a number of different topics. Discussion points included ways of contacting homeworkers, what an organization can offer them, and how to organize homeworkers without risk of losing their work. Another key topic was legislation at national, European, and international levels. Widely different national legislation exists within Europe, with Germany at one end of the scale having comprehensive laws on homework and countries such as Greece and Britain having no specific laws. Enforcement also varies considerably. Another common theme is the internationalization of the economy and the need for cooperation to keep track of production and its movement. In Italy, for example, employers responded to legislation during the 1970s by moving much of the work out of the country. Italian trade unions speak passionately about the need for international cooperation. At the meeting in Thessaloniki, homeworkers and an employer discussed how work was moving to Albania and Greece from other parts of Europe.

In 1995, the European Homeworking Group continued to extend its contacts to new countries. It planned to meet in Madeira, Portugal, and learn more about the work of the union which has organized home-embroiderers there. Other plans included setting up the group on a formal basis, perhaps as a regional sub-group of Homenet International, and lobbying European governments and trade unions for an ILO convention.

The group also supported a planned pilot survey of subcontracting chains and homework in Europe. Grassroots activists and researchers have long known that homeworkers are linked to big companies though long subcontracting chains which cross national boundaries. Homeworkers in Greece, for example, are sewing garments sold in retail stores in Northern Europe. Shoes made at home in Portugal and children's clothes made in the North of England are destined for sale in Germany and elsewhere. Electronic and electrical companies are also organizing their work on a European and often world-wide basis. The survey was designed to document some of these chains in Greece, Italy, Portugal, and UK.

Work at the European level has given the West Yorkshire Homeworking Unit a wider framework within which to operate and make a range of contacts. Homeworkers from West Yorkshire spoke of their own experience of homework at the EU seminar and met others from different countries. As well as building grassroots connections, we are attempting to raise the issue of homework at a number of official levels and to develop a wider program on homework based on the models of ILO regional programs.

At the European level as well as locally there is a need to build alliances to develop projects on homeworking. At the seminar, those active in homeworking were mostly women trade unionists. In the Netherlands, the Women's Union has established its own project on homework and aims to integrate its efforts with the government, employers, and trade unions. In both Greece and Italy, women trade unionists, particularly in the clothing and leather industries, have taken the initiative, often working with sympathetic women researchers or other women's organizations. In Madeira, the trade union has developed its work most extensively over the past seventeen years with thousands of home embroiderers.

Women are likely to play an increasingly important role in the unions as their numbers in the work force of European countries expand. Together with growing concern about telework, it seems likely that there will be a greater interest in new ways of working with "marginal" groups, or those in the informal sector. An international network can make an important contribution to spreading information and experiences.

Conclusion

The West Yorkshire Homeworking Unit has always emphasized direct contact with homeworkers and creating ways of organizing that can empower them through participation in campaigns and other events. The international contacts that we have gained in recent years have fed into the process of building a grassroots organization, giving us inspiration and practical lessons on organizing. This international solidarity has developed through informal networks of women working at the grassroots level, in unions or as researchers.[15]

The Brussels meeting in March 1994 made an important step toward a more formal international network. Coordination in 1994 and 1995 was particularly important in preparation for the ILO conference and the Beijing Women's Conference. But in the longterm, the network should help make homeworking more visible at the international level and give practical assistance, information, and encouragement to those working at the grassroots level.

Notes

1   For detailed information on this conference, see "'Not a Proper Job,'" report of the International Conference on Homeworking, May 7–10, 1990, special issue of *News from IRENE* (Tilburg) 12 (September 1990).

2   For an account of work with homeworkers in the Netherlands, see Jane Tate, "Organizing Homeworkers in the Informal Sector," in *Women in Unions: Organizing the Unorganized*, eds. Margaret Hosmer Martens and Swasti Mitter (Geneva: International Labour Office, 1994), pp. 61–94.

3   For an account of the visit to the Netherlands, see *Outworkers News*, newsletter of

the West Yorkshire Homeworking Group, 5 (January 1991).

4   For more information on the West Yorkshire conference, see "From Gift Tags to Circuit Boards" (Batley: West Yorkshire Homeworking Unit, September 1994).

5   For more details of the visit to Portugal, see *Outworkers News* 12, newsletter of the West Yorkshire Homeworking Group (September 1993).

6   "Black" in the British context includes people from Asia as well as those of African descent.

7   See the newsletter of the Clean Clothes Campaign, *Clean Clothes*, published in 1993 and 1994.

8   See "The Labour Behind the Label," Women Working Worldwide educational pack.

9   See Sheila Rowbotham and Swasti Mitter, eds. *Dignity and Daily Bread: New Forms of Economic Organising Among Poor Women in the Third World and the First* (London: Routledge, 1994).

10 International Labour Organisation, "Social Protection of Homeworkers: Documents of the Meeting of Experts on the Social Protection of Homeworkers" (Geneva: International Labour Office, 1990), p. 93.

11 For more information on the ILO Southeast Asia project, see *Silent No More* (Bangkok: ILO, 1993); also Lucita Lazo, "Women's Empowerment in the Making," in this volume.

12 For details on the work in Australia, see Tate, "Organizing Homeworkers in the Informal Sector."

13 See "From the Double Day to the Endless Day" (Toronto: Canadian Centre for Policy Alternatives, n.d.).

14 See Jane Tate, "Homeworking in EC," report of the ad hoc Working Group on Homeworking (Brussels: European Commission, 1993).

15 For more information on the West Yorkshire Homeworking Unit, see Sheila Rowbotham, *Homeworkers Worldwide* (London: Merlin Press, 1993); and West Yorkshire Homeworking Group, *A Penny a Bag* (Batley: Yorkshire and Humberside Low Pay Unit, 1990).

Bibliography »

Abbott, Edith. *Women in Industry: A Study in American Economic History.* New York: D. Appleton and Co., 1910.

Abreu, Alice Rangel de Paiva. *O Avesso da Moda: Trabalho a Domicílio na Indústria de Confecção.* São Paulo: Hucitec, 1986.

Abreu, Alice Rangel de Paiva and Bila Sorj. "Trabalho a domicílio nas sociedades contemporâneas: Uma revisão da literatura recente." In *O Trabalho Invisível: Estudos sobre trabalho a domicílio no Brasil,* eds. Alice R. de P. Abreu and Bila Sorj. Rio de Janeiro: Rio Fundo, 1993, pp. 11–24.

Afary, Janet. "On the Origins of Feminism in Early 20th-Century Iran." *Journal of Women's History* 1 (Summer 1989): 65–87.

Aguilar, Filomeno and Virginia Miralao. "The Philippines." In *Artisans in Economic Development: Evidence from Asia,* ed. Elwood A. Pye. Ottawa: International Development Research Centre, 1988, pp. 94–121.

Alavi, Hamza. "Formation of the Social Structure of South Asia under the Impact of Colonialism." In *South Asia,* ed. John Harriss. New York: Monthly Review Press, 1989, pp. 5–19.

Alexander, Sally. "Women's Work in Nineteenth-Century London: A Study of the Years 1820–50." In *The Rights and Wrongs of Women,* ed. Juliet Mitchell and Ann Oakley. New York: Penguin, 1976, pp. 59–111.

Allen, Sheila and Carol Wolkowitz. *Homeworking: Myths and Realities.* London: Macmillan, 1987.

Alonso, José. *Mujeres Maquiladoras y Microindustria Domestica.* Mexico, D.F.: Distribuciones Fontamara, 1991.

Anttonen, Anneli et al. *Naisten Hyvinvointivaltio* (Women's Welfare State). Tampere: Vastapaino, 1994.

Ardener, Shirley. "Ground Rules and Social Maps for Women.," In *Women and Space,* ed. Shirley Ardener. New York: St. Martin's Press, 1982, pp. 11–32.

Arias, Patricia. *Guadalajara, la Grand Ciudad de la Pequeña Industria.* Zamora: El Colegio de Michoacan, 1985.

———. *La Nueva Rusticidad Mexicana.* Mexico City: Conaculta, 1992.

"Asian Homeworkers Meet in RP May 10." *News Today* (Manila). 1 May 1991, p.3.

Azari, Farah. ed. *Women of Iran: The Conflict with Fundamentalist Islam.* London: Ithaca Press, 1983.

Banerjee, Nirmala. "Conclusion." In *Indian Women in a Changing Industrial Scenario,* ed. N. Banerjee. New Delhi: Sage Publications, 1991, pp. 299–311.

———. "The More it Changes, the More it is the Same: Women Workers in Export Oriented Industries." In *Indian Women in a Changing Industrial Scenario,* ed. N. Banerjee. New Delhi: Sage Publications, 1991, pp. 237–298.

———. "Small and Large Units: Symbiosis or Matsyanyaya." In *Small Scale Enterprises in Industrial Development: The Indian Experience,* ed. K.B. Suri. New Delhi: Sage Publications, 1988, pp. 184–202.

————. *Women Workers in the Unorganized Sector: The Calcutta Experience.* Hyderabad: Sangram Books, 1985.

————. "Women's Work and Discrimination." In *Tyranny of the Household: Investigative Essays on Women's Work,* ed. Devaki Jain and Nirmala Banerjee. New Delhi: Shakti Books, 1985, pp. 146–191.

————. "Working Women in Colonial Bengal." In *Recasting Women: Essays in Indian Colonial History,* ed. Kumkum Sangari and Sudesh Vaid. New Brunswick: Rutgers University Press, 1990.

Banks, Andy. "The Power and Promise of Community Unionism." *Labor Research Review* 18 (1991).

Barbagelata, H. "Different Categories of Workers and Labour Contracts." In *Comparative Labour Law and Industrial Relations,* ed. R. Blanpain. Deventer, The Netherlands: Kluwer Law and Taxation Publishers, 1987, pp. 427–452.

Bardhan, Kalpana. "Stratification of Women's Work in Rural India: Determinants, Effects, and Strategies." In *Social and Economic Development in India: A Reassessment,* ed. Dilip K. Basu and Richard Sisson. New Delhi: Sage Publications, 1986, pp. 89–105.

Barrett, Michele A. *Women's Oppression Today: Problems in Marxist Feminist Analysis.* London: Verso, 1980.

Basant, Rakesh and B. L. Kumar. "Data Base for Study of Household Manufacturing Sector: Problems of Comparability." *Economic and Political Weekly* 25 (May 19, 1990): p. 1083.

Baud, Isa. *Forms of Production and Women's Labor: Gender Aspects of Industrialisation in India and Mexico.* New Delhi: Sage Publications, 1992.

Bauer, Janet. "Demographic Change, Women and the Family in a Migrant Neighborhood of Tehran." In *Women and the Family in Iran,* ed. Asghar Fathi. Leiden, Netherlands: E.J. Brill, 1985, pp. 158–186.

Beck, Lois. "Women among Qashqa'i Nomadic Pastoralists in Iran." In *Women in the Muslim World,* eds. Lois Beck and Nikki Keddie. Cambridge: Harvard University Press, 1987.

Beechey, Veronica. "On Patriarchy." *Feminist Review* 3 (1979): 66–82.

Benería, Lourdes. "Accounting for Women's Work." In *Women and Development: The Sexual Division of Labor in Rural Societies,* ed. Lourdes Beneria. New York: Praeger Publishers, 1982, pp. 119–147.

————. "The Mexican Debt Crisis: Restructuring in the Economy and the Household." In *Unequal Burden: Economic Crises, Persistent Poverty, and Women's Work,* eds. Lourdes Benería and Shelley Feldman. Boulder: Westview Press, pp. 83–104.

————. "Production, Reproduction, and the Sexual Division of Labor." *Cambridge Journal of Economics* 3 (September 1979): 203–25.

Benería, Lourdes and Shelley Feldman, eds. *Unequal Burden: Economic Crises, Persistent Poverty, and Women's Work.* Boulder: Westview Press, 1992.

Benería, Lourdes and Martha Roldán. *The Crossroads of Class and Gender: Industrial Homework, Subcontracting, and Household Dynamics in Mexico City.* Chicago: The University of Chicago Press, 1987.

Benería, Lourdes and Gita Sen. "Accumulation, Reproduction, and Women's Role in Economic Development: Boserup Revisited." *Signs: A Journal of Women in Culture and Society* 7 (Winter 1981): 279–298.

Benería, Lourdes and Catharine R. Stimpson, eds. *Women, Households, and the Economy.* New Brunswick: Rutgers University Press, 1987.

Berger, Marguerite. "An Introduction." In *Women's Ventures: Assistance to the Informal Sector in Latin America*, ed. Marguerite Berger and Mayra Buvinic. West Hartford: Kumarian Press, 1989, pp. 1–18.

Berik, Günseli. *Women Carpet Weavers in Rural Turkey: Patterns of Employment, Earnings and Status.* Geneva: International Labour Office, 1987.

Bhatt, Ela. "The Invisibility of Home-Based Work: The Case of Piece Rate Workers in India." In *Invisible Hands: Women in Home-Based Production*, eds. Andrea M. Singh and Anita Kelles-Viitanen. New Delhi: Sage Publications, 1987, pp. 29–34.

———. "Toward Empowerment." *World Development* 17 (July 1989): 1059–1065.

Bhattacharya, B. B. and Arup Mitra. "Employment and Structural Adjustment: A Look at 1991 Census Data." *Economic and Political Weekly* 28 (September 18, 1993): 1989–1995.

Bhatty, Zarina. *The Economic Role and Status of Women in the Beedi Industry in Allahabad, India.* Saarbrücken, Fort Lauderdale: Verlag Breitenbach Publishers, 1981.

Bisset, Liz and Ursula Huws. *Sweated Labour: Homeworking in Britain Today.* Nottingham: Low Pay Unit, 1985.

Black, Clementina. *Home Industries of Women in London, 1897: Report of an Inquiry into Thirty-Five Trades.* London: The Women's Industrial Council, 1897.

Blewett, Mary. *Men, Women, and Work: Class, Gender, and Protest in the New England Shoe Industry, 1790–1910.* Urbana: University of Illinois Press, 1988.

Blumberg, Rae. "Income under Female versus Male Control: Hypotheses from a Theory of Gender Stratification and Data from the Third World." In *Gender, Family and Economy*, ed. Rae Blumberg. Newbury Park: Sage Publications, 1991, pp. 97–127.

———. "Towards a Feminist Theory of Development." In Ruth A. Wallace, ed., *Feminism and Sociological Theory.* London: Sage Publications, 1989, pp. 161–199.

Boomgard, James J. "A.I.D. Microenterprise Stocktaking: Synthesis Report." A.I.D. Evaluation Special Study No. 65. Washington, D.C.: U.S. Agency for International Development, 1989.

Booth, Anne and Konta Damanik. "Central Java and Yogyakarta: Malthus Overcome?" In *Unity and Diversity, Regional Economic Development in Indonesia since 1970*, ed. Hall Hill. Singapore: Oxford University Press, 1989, pp. 283–306.

Boris, Eileen. *Home to Work: Motherhood and the Politics of Industrial Homework in the United States.* New York: Cambridge University Press, 1994.

———. "Homework and Women's Rights: The Case of the Vermont Knitters, 1980–1985." *Signs* 13 (Autumn 1987): 98–120.

Boris, Eileen and Cynthia R. Daniels. *Homework: Historical and Contemporary Perspectives on Paid Labor at Home.* Urbana: University of Illinois Press, 1989.

Boserup, Ester. *Women's Role in Economic Development.* New York: St. Martin's Press, 1970.

Boxer, Marilyn. "Protective Legislation and Home Industry: The Marginalization of Women Workers in Late Nineteenth-Early Twentieth Century France." *Journal of Social History* 20 (Fall 1986): 45–65.

———. "Women in Industrial Homework: The Flowermakers of Paris in the Belle Epoque." *French Historical Studies* 12 (Spring 1982): 401–423.

Boydston, Jeanne. *Home and Work: Housework, Wages, and the Ideology of Labor in the Early Republic.* New York: Oxford University Press, 1990.

Boyolali, Kabupat. "Central Java." *Bulletin of Indonesian Economic Studies* 25, 2 (1989): 79–99.

Bromley, Ray and Chris Gerry. "Who are the Casual Poor?" In *Casual Work and Poverty in Third World Cities,* ed. Ray Bromley and Chris Gerry. Chichester: John Wiley and Sons, 1979, pp. 3–23.

Brown, Simon. Paper presented at the International Conference on Homeworking, May 7–10, 1990, Helvoirt, The Netherlands, n.p.

Bruschini, Cristina. "Crescimento e Crise: trabalho das brasileiras, paulistas e nordestinas, de 1970 a 1985." *Ciência e Cultura* 42, 3/4 (March/April 1990): 226–247.

Butler, Judith. *Gender Trouble: Feminism and the Subversion of Identity.* New York: Routledge, 1990.

Buvinic, Mayra, Marguerite Berger, and Cecilia Jaramillo. "Impact of a Credit Project for Women and Men Microentrepreneurs in Quito, Ecuador." In *Women's Ventures: Assistance to the Informal Sector in Latin America,* ed. Marguerite Berger and Mayra Buvinic. West Hartford: Kumarian Press, 1989, pp. 222–246.

Buvinic, Mayra, Margaret Lycette, and William McGreevey, eds. *Women and Poverty in the Third World.* Baltimore: The Johns Hopkins University Press, 1983.

Cabanes, Robert. "Filières et stratégies socio-professionnelles (Étude de cas de douze ouvriers à São Paulo, Brésil)." *Cahiers des Sciences Humaines,* 23,2 (1987): 163–181.

Calman, Leslie J. *Toward Empowerment: Women and Movement Politics in India.* Boulder: Westview Press, 1992.

Cameron, Barbara and Teresa Mak. "Working Conditions of Chinese-Speaking Homeworkers in the Toronto Garment Industry: Summary of the Results of a Survey Conducted by the ILGWU." Mimeo.

Características Sociais dos Trabalhadores Informais: O caso das Áreas Metropolitanas no Brasil." *Estudos Afro Asiáticos* 19 (1990): 61–80.

Castells, Manuel and Alejandro Portes. "World Underneath: The Origins, Dynamics, and Effects of the Informal Economy." In *The Informal Economy: Studies in Advanced and Less Developed Countries,* eds. Alejandro Portes, Manuel Castells, and Lauren A. Benton. Baltimore: The Johns Hopkins University Press, 1989: 11–37.

Chaney, Elsa and Marianne Schmink. "Women and Modernization: Access to Tools." In *Sex and Class in Latin America,* eds. June Nash and Helen Safa. New York: Bergin and Garvey, 1980.

Chant, Silvia. *Women and Survival in Mexican Cities: Perspectives on Gender, Labor Markets and Low-Income Households.* New York: Manchester University Press, 1991.

Charlton, Sue Ellen M. *Women in Third World Development.* Boulder: Westview, 1984.

Chatterjee, Somnath and Rakesh Mohan. "India's Garment Exports." *Economic and Political Weekly* 28 (August 28, 1993), M-95–M-119.

Chen, Marty. "The Working Women's Forum: Organizing for Credit and Change." In *SEEDS: Supporting Women's Work in the Third World*, ed. Ann Leonard (New York: Feminist Press, 1989), pp. 51–72.

Chossudovsky, Michael. "India Under IMF Rule." *Economic and Political Weekly* 28 (March 6, 1993), pp. 385f.

Christensen, Kathleen. "Home-Based Clerical Work: No Simple Truth, No Single Reality." In *Homework: Historical and Contemporary Perspectives on Paid Labor at Home*, eds. Eileen Boris and Cynthia R. Daniels. Urbana and Chicago: University of Illinois Press, 1989, pp.183–197.

———. "Independent Contracting." In *The New Era of Home-Based Work: Directions and Policies*, ed. Kathleen Christensen (Boulder: Westview, 1988), pp. 79–91.

———. *Women and Home-Based Work: The Unspoken Contract*. New York: Henry Holt, 1988.

Churchryk, Patricia M. "Subversive Mothers: The Women's Opposition to the Military Regime in Chile." In *Women, the State, and Development*, eds. Sue Ellen M. Charlton, Jana Everett, and Kathleen Staudt. Albany: State University of New York Press, 1989, pp. 130–151.

"The Cigar-Makers' Strike." *New York World*, Nov. 9, 1877.

Clark, Christopher. *The Roots of Rural Capitalism: Western Massachusetts, 1780–1860.* Ithaca, N.Y.: Cornell Univ. Press, 1990.

Coffin, Judith. "Social Science Meets Sweated Labor: Reinterpreting Women's Work in Late Nineteenth-Century France." *Journal of Modern History* 63 (June 1991): 237–243.

Collins, Jane L. and Martha Gimenez, eds. *Work Without Wages: Domestic Labor and Self-Employment Within Capitalism*. Albany: State University of New York Press, 1990.

Cook, Scott. "Craft Commodity Production, Market Diversity, and Differential Rewards in Mexican Capitalism Today." In *Crafts in the World Market: The Impact of Global Exchange on Middle American Artisans*, ed. June Nash. Albany: State University of New York Press, pp. 59–83.

Coons, Lorraine. "'Neglected Sisters' of the Women's Movement: The Perception and Experience of Working Mothers in the Parisian Garment Industry, 1860–1915." *Journal of Women's History* 5 (Fall 1993): 56–59.

———. *Women Home Workers in the Parisian Garment Industry, 1860–1915*. New York: Garland Publishing, Inc., 1987.

Córdova, Efrén. "From Full-time Wage Employment to Atypical Employment: A Major Shift in the Evolution of Labour Relations?" *International Labour Review* 125 (November-December 1986), 641–657.

Coser, Lewis A. and Rose Laub Coser. "The Housewife and Her 'Greedy Family'." In *Greedy Institutions: Patterns of Undivided Commitment*, ed. Lewis A. Coser. New York: The Free Press, 1974, pp. 89–100.

Costello, Cynthia and Anne J. Stone, eds. *The American Woman, 1994–95: Where We Stand.*

New York: Norton, 1994.

Crummett, Maria de los Angeles. "Rural Women and Industrial Home Work in Latin America: Research Review and Agenda." World Employment Programme Research Working Paper. Geneva: International Labour Organisation, 1988.

Dahlström, Edmund. "Everyday-Life Theories and Their Historical and Ideological Contexts." In *The Multiparadigmatic Trend in Sociology*, ed. Ulf Himmelstrand. Uppsala: Almqvist & Wiksell, 1987, pp. 93–114.

Dangler, Jamie Faricellia. *Hidden in the Home: The Role of Waged Homework in the Modern World Economy*. Albany: State University of New York Press, 1994.

———. "Industrial Homework in the Modern World-Economy." *Contemporary Crises* 10 (1986): 259–264.

Datar, Chhaya. *Waging Change: Women Tobacco Workers in Nipani Organize*. New Delhi: Kali for Women, 1989.

Dauber, Roslyn and Melinda L. Cain, eds. *Women and Technological Change in Developing Countries*. Boulder: Westview, 1981.

Daines, Victoria and David Seddon. "Confronting Austerity: Women's Responses to Economic Reform." In *Women's Lives and Public Policy: The International Experience*, eds. Meredeth Turshen and Briavel Hocomb (Westport: Praeger, 1993), pp. 3–32.

Davidson, Osha Gray. *Broken Heartland: The Rise of America's Rural Ghetto*. New York and Toronto: The Free Press, 1990.

Davidson, Patricia. "Comment: The Definition of 'Employee' under Title VII: Distinguishing Between Employees and Independent Contractors." *University of Cincinnati Law Review* 53 (1984): 203–229.

Davies, Karen. *Women and Time: Weaving the Strands of Everyday Life*. Lund: Grahns boktryckeri, 1989.

Deshpande, Sudha and L.K. Deshpande. "New Economic Policy and Female Employment." *Economic and Political Weekly* 27 (October 10, 1992): 2248–1149.

Dhamija, Jasleen. "Women and Handicrafts: Myth and Reality." In *SEEDS: Supporting Women's Work in the Third World*, ed. Ann Leonard (New York: Feminist Press, 1989), pp. 195–212.

Dharmalingam, A. "Female Beedi Workers in a South Indian Village." *Economic and Political Weekly* 28 (July 3–10, 1993): 1461–1468.

Directory of Labor Organizations in Canada. Ottawa: Ministry of Supplies and Services, 1992.

"DOLE Pushes Legislation for Homeworkers." *Businessworld* (Manila) 10 April 1991, p. 11.

"Drilon Appeals for Welfare of Homeworkers." *The Manila Chronicle* (Manila) 7 October 1989, p. 3.

"Drilon Vows to Protect Homeworkers." *Manila Bulletin* (Manila) 7 October 1989, pp. 1 and 20.

"Drilon Wants Protection for 7M Home Workers." *Business World* (Manila) 9 October 1989, p. 11.

Dublin, Thomas. "Rural Putting-Out Work in Early Nineteenth-Century New

England: Women and the Transition to Capitalism in the Countryside." *New England Quarterly* 64 (1991): 531–573.

Eber, Christine and Brenda Rosenbaum. "'That we may serve beneath your hands and feet': Women Weavers in Highland Chiapas, Mexico." In *Crafts in the World Market: The Impact of Global Exchange on Middle American Artisans*, ed. June Nash. Albany: State University of New York Press, 1992, pp. 155–179.

Eisenstein, Zillah R. "Developing a Theory of Capitalist Patriarchy." In *Capitalist Patriarchy and the Case for Socialist Feminism*, ed. Zillah R. Eisenstein. New York: Monthly Review Press, 1979.

Elisburg, Donald. "Legalities." *Telematics and Informatics* 2 (1985): 181–185.

Elling, Monica. *På tröskeln till ett nytt liv?* (On the threshold to a new life?) Göteborg, Sweden: Arbetslivscentrum, 1984.

Elling, Monica and Marianne Parmsund. *Långt borta och nära: Om distansarbete på kontorsområdet.* (Far away and nearby: On distance work in office work) Göteborg, Sweden: Arbetslivscentrum, 1982.

Elson, Diane. "From Survival Strategies to Transformation Strategies: Women's Needs and Structural Adjustment." In *Unequal Burden: Economic Crises, Persistent Poverty, and Women's Work*, eds. Lourdes Benería and Shelley Feldman. Boulder: Westview Press, pp. 26–48.

Elson, Diane and Ruth Pearson. "Nimble Fingers Make Cheap Workers: An Analysis of Women's Employment in Third World Export Manufacturing." *Feminist Review* 7 (Spring 1981): 87–107.

English, Paul. *City and Village in Iran: Settlement and Economy In Kirman Basin.* Madison: University of Wisconsin Press, 1966.

Espinal, Rosario and Sherri Grasmuck. "Gender, Households and Informal Entrepreneurship in the Dominican Republic." Paper presented at the Sixth International Forum, Association for Women in Development, October 21–24, 1993.

Fathi, Asghar, ed. *Women and the Family in Iran.* Leiden, The Netherlands: E.J. Brill, 1985.

Feldman, Shelley. "Still Invisible: Women in the Informal Sector." In *The Women and International Development Annual*, Vol. 2., ed. Rita Gallin and Anne Ferguson. Boulder: Westview Press, 1991, pp. 59–86.

Ferdows, Adel K. and Amir H. Ferdows. "Women in Shi'i Figh: Images Through the Hadith." In *Women and Revolution in Iran*, ed. Gity Nashat. Boulder: Westview, 1983.

Fernandes, Rubem César. *Censo Institucional Evangélico - CIN.* Rio de Janeiro: Núcleo de Pesquisas do ISER, 1992.

Fernea, Elizabeth. *A Street in Marrakech.* Anchor Books, 1980.

Finance Division, Government of Pakistan. *Economic Survey, 1992–93.* Islamabad: Economic Adviser's Wing, July 1993.

Fitchen, Janet. *Endangered Spaces, Enduring Places: Change, Identity, and Survival in Rural America.* Boulder: Westview Press, 1991.

Forester, Tom. *High-Tech Society: The Story of the Information Technology Revolution.* Oxford: Basil Blackwell, 1987.

————. "The Myth of the Electronic Cottage." *Futures* 3 (June 1988): 227–240.

Fortuna, Juan Carlos and Suzana Prates. "Informal Sector versus Informalized Labor Relations in Uruguay." In *The Informal Economy: Studies in Advanced and Less Developed Countries*, ed. Alejandro Portes, Manuel Castells and Lauren Benton. Baltimore: The Johns Hopkins University Press, 1989, pp. 78–94.

Frader, Laura Levine. "Women in the Industrial Capitalist Economy." In *Becoming Visible: Women in European History*, eds. Renate Bridenthal, Claudia Koonz, and Susan Stuard, 2nd edition. Boston: Houghton Mifflin Co, 1987, pp. 309–333.

Franzoi, Barbara. "'…with the wolf always at the door…': Women's Work in Domestic Industry in Britain and Germany." In *Connecting Spheres: Women in the Western World, 1500 to the Present*, ed. Marilyn J. Boxer and Jean H. Quataert. New York: Oxford University Press, 1987, pp. 146–155.

————. *At the Very Least She Pays the Rent: Women and German Industrialization, 1871–1914.* Westport, Conn.: Greenwood Press, 1985.

Friberg, Tora. *Kvinnors vardag: Om kvinnors arbete och liv. Anpassningsstrategier i tid och rum.* (Women's everyday: on women's work and life. Coping strategies in time and space). Lund: Lund University Press, 1990.

Friedberger, Mark. *Farm Families and Change in Twentieth Century America.* Lexington: The University Press of Kentucky, 1988.

Friedl, Erika. *Women of Deh Koh: Lives in an Iranian Village.* New York: Penguin, 1989.

Fröbel, Folker, Otto Kreye, and Jürgen Heinrichs. *The New International Division of Labour: Structural Unemployment in Industrialised Countries and Industrialisation in Developing Countries.* Trans. Pete Burgess. Cambridge: Cambridge University Press, 1980.

"From the Double Day to the Endless Day." Toronto: Canadian Centre for Policy Alternatives, n.d.

"From Gift Tags to Circuit Boards." Batley: West Yorkshire Homeworking Unit, September 1994.

Fuziah, Raja and Ismail Rejab. "Malaysia." In *Artisans in Economic Development: Evidence from Asia*, ed. Elwood A. Pye. Ottawa: International Development Research Centre, 1988, pp. 81–93.

Gallin, Rita. "Women and the Export Industry in Taiwan: The Muting of Class Consciousness." In *Women Workers and Global Restructuring*, ed. Kathryn Ward. Ithaca: ILR Press, 1990, pp. 179–192.

Geertz, Clifford. *Agricultural Involution, the Process of Ecological Change in Indonesia.* Berkeley: University of California Press, 1968.

Gender and Poverty in India: A World Bank Country Study. Washington, D.C.: The World Bank, 1991.

Glader, Jeanne M. "Harvest of Shame: The Imposition of Independent Contractor Status on Migrant Farmworkers and Its Ramifications for Migrant Children." *Hastings Law Journal* 42 (July 1992): 1455–1490.

Gladhart, Peter Michael and Emily Winter Gladhart. "Northern Ecuador's Sweater Industry: Rural Women's Contribution to Economic Development." Michigan